THE 7 CONTINENTS

ANTARCTICA

MW01195679

CONTENTS

Downloadable Maps

Five maps used in this book are available for download on our Web site, as well as two color maps: one projection map of the world and one map of Antarctica.

How to Download:

1. Go to www.evan-moor.com/resources.
2. Enter your e-mail address and the resource code for this product—EMC3736.
3. You will receive an e-mail with a link to the downloadable maps.

What's in This Book

▶ **5 sections** of reproducible information and activity pages centered on five main topics: Antarctica in the World, Physical Features, History of Exploration, Antarctica Today, and Wildlife.

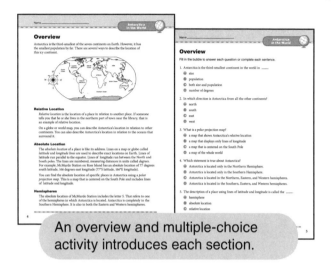

An overview and multiple-choice activity introduces each section.

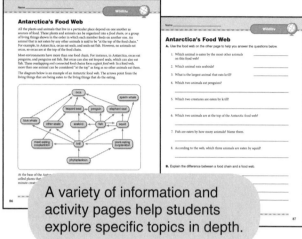

A variety of information and activity pages help students explore specific topics in depth.

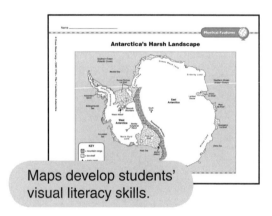

Maps develop students' visual literacy skills.

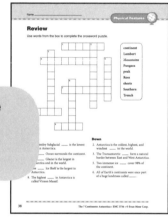

A crossword puzzle at the end of each section provides a fun review activity.

▶ **1 section** of assessment activities

▶ **1 section** of open-ended note takers

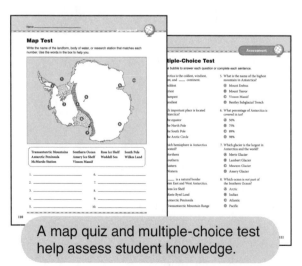

A map quiz and multiple-choice test help assess student knowledge.

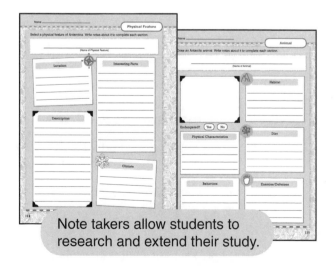

Note takers allow students to research and extend their study.

Antarctica in the World

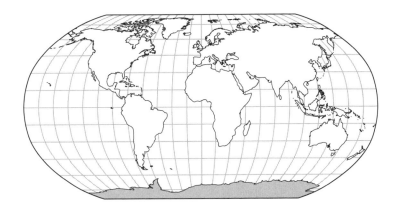

This section introduces students to the location of Antarctica in the world. Students learn about the difference between relative and absolute location, as well as the hemispheres in which Antarctica lies. Students also practice using lines of latitude and longitude to find places on a map and learn about polar projections.

Each skill in this section is based on the following National Geography Standards:

Essential Element 1: The World in Spatial Terms

Standard 1: How to use maps and other geographic representations, tools, and technologies to acquire, process, and report information from a spatial perspective

CONTENTS

Overview

Antarctica is the third-smallest of the seven continents on Earth. However, it has the smallest population by far. There are several ways to describe the location of this icy continent.

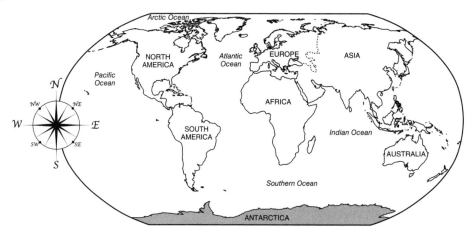

Relative Location

Relative location is the location of a place in relation to another place. If someone tells you that he or she lives in the northern part of town near the library, that is an example of relative location.

On a globe or world map, you can describe Antarctica's location in relation to other continents. You can also describe Antarctica's location in relation to the oceans that surround it.

Absolute Location

The *absolute location* of a place is like its address. Lines on a map or globe called *latitude* and *longitude lines* are used to describe exact locations on Earth. Lines of latitude run parallel to the equator. Lines of longitude run between the North and South poles. The lines are numbered, measuring distances in units called *degrees*. For example, McMurdo Station on Ross Island has an absolute location of 77 degrees south latitude, 166 degrees east longitude (77°S latitude, 166°E longitude).

You can find the absolute location of specific places in Antarctica using a *polar projection map*. This is a map that is centered on the South Pole and includes lines of latitude and longitude.

Hemispheres

The absolute location of McMurdo Station includes the letter *S*. That refers to one of the hemispheres in which Antarctica is located. Antarctica is completely in the Southern Hemisphere. It is also in both the Eastern and Western hemispheres.

Overview

Fill in the bubble to answer each question or complete each sentence.

1. Antarctica is the third-smallest continent in the world in ____.

    Ⓐ size

    Ⓑ population

    Ⓒ both size and population

    Ⓓ number of degrees

2. In which direction is Antarctica from all the other continents?

    Ⓐ north

    Ⓑ south

    Ⓒ east

    Ⓓ west

3. What is a polar projection map?

    Ⓐ a map that shows Antarctica's relative location

    Ⓑ a map that displays only lines of longitude

    Ⓒ a map that is centered on the South Pole

    Ⓓ a map of the whole world

4. Which statement is true about Antarctica?

    Ⓐ Antarctica is located only in the Northern Hemisphere.

    Ⓑ Antarctica is located only in the Southern Hemisphere.

    Ⓒ Antarctica is located in the Northern, Eastern, and Western hemispheres.

    Ⓓ Antarctica is located in the Southern, Eastern, and Western hemispheres.

5. The description of a place using lines of latitude and longitude is called the ____.

    Ⓐ hemisphere

    Ⓑ absolute location

    Ⓒ relative location

    Ⓓ degree

Antarctica's Relative Location

Relative location is the position of a place in relation to another place. How would you describe where Antarctica is located in the world using relative location?

Look at the world map on the other page. One way to describe Antarctica's relative location is to name the other continents that are near it. For example, Antarctica is south of South America, Africa, and Australia.

Another way to describe the relative location of Antarctica is to name the oceans that border the continent. The frigid Southern Ocean surrounds Antarctica. You could also say that the southern parts of the Pacific, Atlantic, and Indian oceans (which make up the Southern Ocean) border Antarctica.

A. Use the information on this page and the map on the other page to complete the paragraphs about the relative location of Antarctica.

    The three continents closest to Antarctica are _____,

Africa, and Australia. Antarctica is located _____ of all of

these continents. It is even farther south of the continents of _____,

Asia, and Europe.

    Antarctica is also bordered by the _____ Ocean

on all sides. This ocean is made up of the southern parts of the Atlantic,

_____, and Indian oceans.

B. Use colored pencils to fill in the map on the other page according to the directions below.

1. Color the small island continent north of Antarctica orange.

2. Use blue to circle the name of the ocean that surrounds Antarctica.

3. Draw a snake on the continent that is closest to Antarctica.

Antarctica's Relative Location

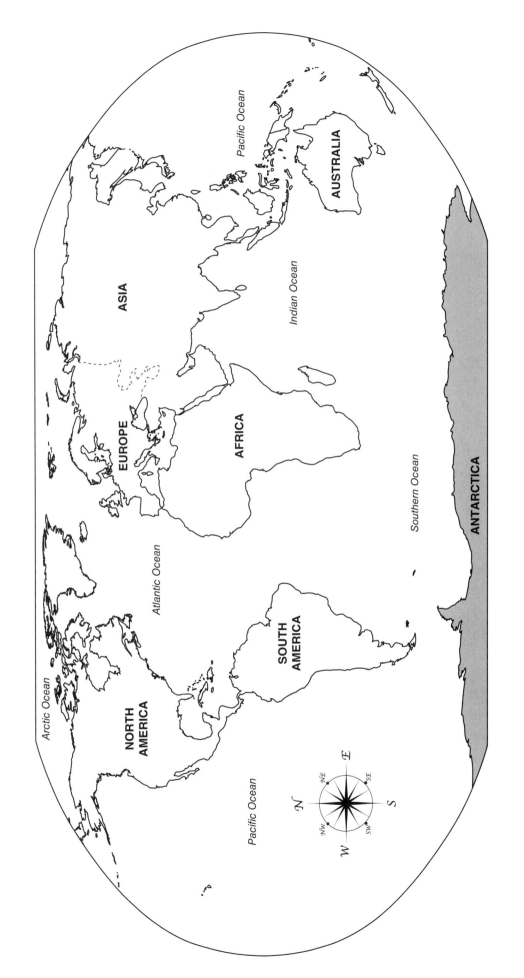

Pacific Ocean

ASIA

AUSTRALIA

Indian Ocean

EUROPE

AFRICA

Arctic Ocean

Atlantic Ocean

Southern Ocean

ANTARCTICA

NORTH
AMERICA

SOUTH
AMERICA

Pacific Ocean

N NE
NW
W   E
SW   SE
S

Antarctica's Hemispheres

On a globe, Earth is divided into four hemispheres by a horizontal line called the *equator* and by vertical lines that run from the North Pole to the South Pole. The hemispheres are the Northern, Southern, Western, and Eastern. All of Antarctica is in the Southern Hemisphere because the entire continent is south of the equator. Antarctica is also in both the Eastern and Western hemispheres.

Northern and Southern Hemispheres

A globe shows an imaginary horizontal line that runs around the center of Earth. This line is called the equator. The equator divides Earth into the Northern and Southern hemispheres.

Since Antarctica is south of the equator, the continent is in the Southern Hemisphere.

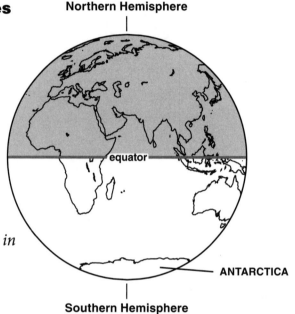

Eastern and Western Hemispheres

A globe also shows imaginary vertical lines that run from the North Pole to the South Pole, the southernmost point on Earth. One of these lines is called the *prime meridian*. This line, along with its twin line on the opposite side of the globe, create the Western and Eastern hemispheres.

Since the prime meridian runs through the middle of Antarctica, the continent is in both the Eastern and Western hemispheres.

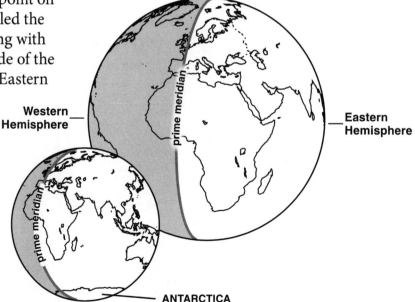

Antarctica's Hemispheres

A. Write the letter of the definition that matches each term. Use the information and the globe pictures on the other page to help you.

_____ 1. Antarctica

_____ 2. continent

_____ 3. globe

_____ 4. equator

_____ 5. Eastern Hemisphere

_____ 6. hemisphere

_____ 7. South Pole

_____ 8. Southern Hemisphere

_____ 9. prime meridian

_____ 10. Western Hemisphere

a. an imaginary line that runs from the North Pole to the South Pole

b. half of Earth

c. a continent that is in the Southern, Western, and Eastern hemispheres

d. the hemisphere that is west of the prime meridian

e. an imaginary line that divides Earth into the Northern and Southern hemispheres

f. any of the seven large landmasses of Earth

g. the southernmost point on Earth

h. a round model of Earth

i. the hemisphere that is south of the equator

j. the hemisphere that is east of the prime meridian

B. Label the parts of the globe. Use the letters next to the terms in the box.

A. **Southern Hemisphere**

B. **Antarctica**

C. **Western Hemisphere**

D. **Eastern Hemisphere**

E. **equator**

F. **prime meridian**

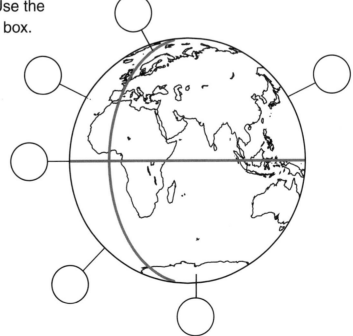

Antarctica's Absolute Location

Many globes contain lines that make it easier to find specific places on Earth. Lines of latitude measure the distance north and south of the equator. Lines of longitude measure the distance east and west of the prime meridian. You can use lines of latitude and longitude to find the absolute location of Antarctica on a globe.

Latitude

The equator is found at the absolute location of 0° (zero degrees) latitude. Other lines of latitude run parallel to the equator and are labeled with an *N* or *S*, depending on whether they are north or south of the equator. Latitude lines are also called *parallels*.

On the picture of the globe, notice the lines of latitude, which run in circles that get farther and farther from the equator and closer to the South Pole. Since all of Antarctica is south of the equator, all of the latitude lines used to find the absolute location of places in Antarctica are labeled in *degrees south*, or °S.

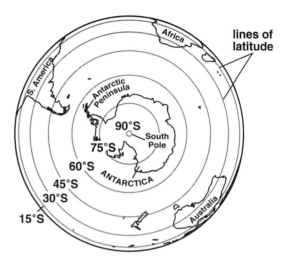

Lines of Latitude (Parallels)

Longitude

The prime meridian runs from the North Pole to the South Pole at 0° (zero degrees) longitude. Other lines of longitude run north and south, too, and are labeled with an *E* or *W*, depending on whether they are east or west of the prime meridian. Longitude lines are also called *meridians*.

On the picture of the globe, notice the lines of longitude. All of them run through Antarctica, meeting at the South Pole. Since half of the continent is east of the prime meridian and its twin line at 180°, half of the longitude lines used to find the absolute location of places in Antarctica are labeled in *degrees east*, or °E. The other half are labeled in *degrees west*, or °W.

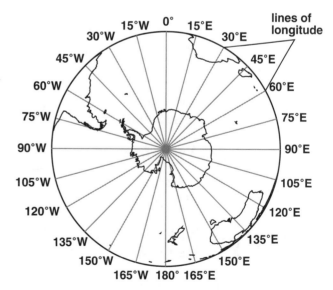

Lines of Longitude (Meridians)

Antarctica's Absolute Location

To find the absolute location of a place, read the latitude line first and then read the longitude line. For example, the latitude 70°S runs through the Antarctic Peninsula. The longitude 65°W also runs through the peninsula. So the absolute location of the Antarctic Peninsula is 70°S latitude, 65°W longitude.

A. Circle the correct answer to each question. Use the pictures of the globes and information on the other page to help you.

1. Which line is at 0 degrees latitude?	**equator**	**prime meridian**
2. Which line runs north and south?	**equator**	**prime meridian**
3. In which direction is Antarctica from the equator?	**north**	**south**
4. Which line of latitude runs through Antarctica?	**75°S**	**60°S**
5. Where is the South Pole located?	**90°S**	**90°N**
6. Which lines run parallel to the equator?	**latitude lines**	**longitude lines**
7. How many degrees are between each line of latitude and longitude on the globe pictures?	**10 degrees**	**15 degrees**
8. What is another name for *lines of latitude*?	**meridians**	**parallels**
9. What is another name for *lines of longitude*?	**parallels**	**meridians**

B. Using the information on this page and the other page, explain why the Antarctic Peninsula has an absolute location labeled in degrees south and west.

_____

_____

Name _____

Using a Polar Projection Map

How do you draw a picture of a round object, like Earth, on a flat piece of paper? In order to show Earth's curved surface on a map, mapmakers use a system called *projection*. In the case of Antarctica, the projection map shows land and water in relation to a central point: the South Pole. This type of map is called a polar projection map. Land near the South Pole is shown accurately. However, as you move farther away from the central point, the size and shape of the land and water become more and more distorted.

A polar projection map also shows lines of latitude and longitude. Study the polar projection map on the other page. Notice the lines of latitude and longitude. You can use these lines to find the absolute location of a specific place in Antarctica. For example, the *r* in the label *Antarctica* is located at 75°S latitude, 45°E longitude.

A. Read each statement. Circle **yes** if it is true or **no** if it is false. Use the map on the other page to help you.

1. The prime meridian runs through Antarctica.   Yes   No

2. All of Antarctica is located between the longitudes of 60°E and 150°E.   Yes   No

3. All of Antarctica is located between the latitudes of 60°S and 90°S.   Yes   No

4. Antarctica is the only continent on the latitude of 75°S.   Yes   No

5. Antarctica shares some of the same south latitude lines with other continents.   Yes   No

6. All of the east and west longitude lines run through Antarctica.   Yes   No

7. The latitude line 90°N runs through Antarctica.   Yes   No

8. Part of Antarctica is located on the latitude line 45°S.   Yes   No

9. There are no continents on 60°S latitude.   Yes   No

B. What is a polar projection map?

_____

_____

Using a Polar Projection Map

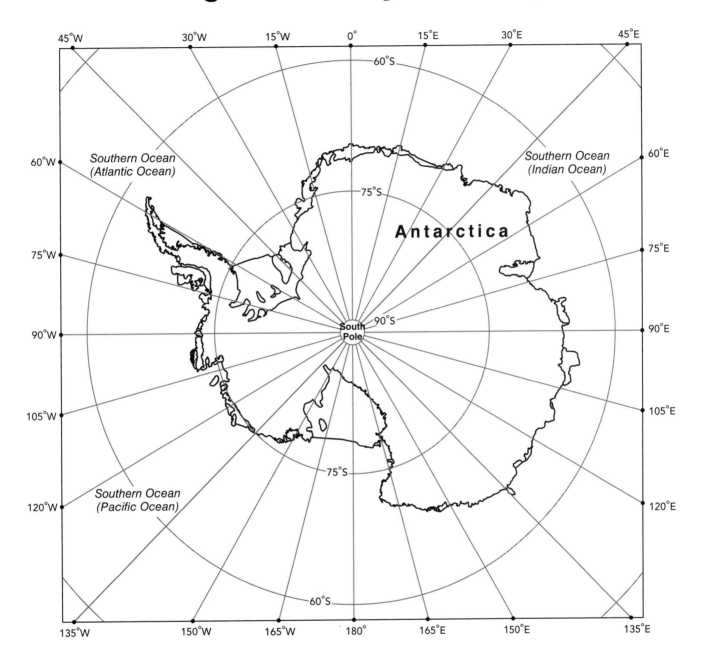

Name _____

Review

Use words from the box to complete the crossword puzzle.

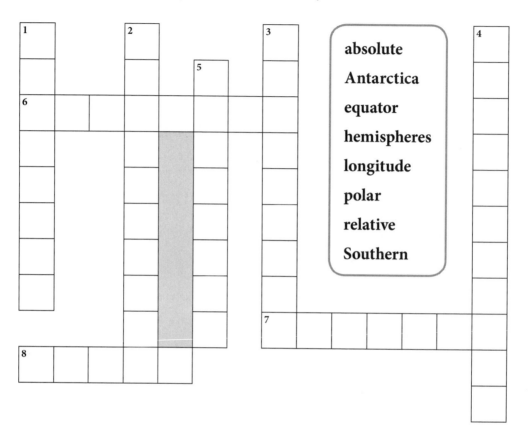

absolute

Antarctica

equator

hemispheres

longitude

polar

relative

Southern

Across

6. Antarctica is surrounded by the _____ Ocean.

7. The _____ is an imaginary line that divides Earth into the Northern and Southern hemispheres.

8. A _____ projection map of Antarctica shows land and water in relation to the South Pole.

Down

1. You can find the _____ location of a place using lines of latitude and longitude.

2. _____ has the smallest population of all the continents.

3. All of the _____ lines on a map meet in Antarctica.

4. Antarctica is in both the Eastern and Western _____.

5. The _____ location of a place is its position in relation to another place.

Physical Features of Antarctica

This section introduces students to the highest, driest, coldest, and iciest continent on the planet. Students discover that Antarctica is covered by thick ice sheets, glaciers, and ice shelves, and that there are mountains above and below the ice. They learn that the Southern Ocean and the seas that are part of it surround the continent. They also study the climate of Antarctica and learn about the effects of climate change.

Each skill in this section is based on the following National Geography Standards:

Essential Element 2: Places and Regions

Standard 4: The physical and human characteristics of places

Essential Element 3: Physical Systems

Standards 7 & 8: The physical processes that shape the patterns of Earth's surface, and the characteristics and spatial distribution of ecosystems on Earth's surface

CONTENTS

Overview

Antarctica is an ice-covered continent on which the South Pole is located. It is the third-smallest continent in the world—about the size of the United States and Mexico put together. Its shape is mostly circular, with a large curving peninsula in the northwest. Antarctica is cut off from the rest of the continents by the Southern Ocean.

Landforms

Two giant regions of ice cover most of Antarctica. These *ice sheets* represent 90% of the world's ice and hold 70% of the world's fresh water.

The Transantarctic Mountain Range divides the continent into the regions of East and West Antarctica. Some of the mountain peaks rise more than 14,000 feet (4,300 m). The mountains have large, ice-free, rocky areas known as *dry valleys*. The valleys were carved by *glaciers,* masses of ice and snow that move slowly down the mountainsides.

East Antarctica is an icy plateau that is about 10,000 feet (3,000 m) above sea level. West Antarctica has both the lowest and highest points on the continent. However, the lowest places are located deep under the ice sheet.

The Antarctic Peninsula is a mountainous region that juts out from West Antarctica and reaches toward the southern tip of South America. Several small islands lie near the peninsula.

Coastal Waters

Antarctica is surrounded by the southern parts of the Atlantic, Pacific, and Indian oceans, which together are called the Southern Ocean. Several major seas, including the Amundsen, Bellingshausen, Davis, Ross, and Weddell seas, are located off the coasts of the continent. *Ice shelves,* large portions of ice sheets that flow onto the ocean's surface, fill several bays and waterways along the coasts.

Climate

Antarctica's climate varies from extreme cold and dry conditions inland to slightly milder and wetter conditions along the coasts. Scientists call the interior of Antarctica a "polar desert" since it gets less than 2 inches (5 cm) of snowfall a year. Coastal areas average about 24 inches (61 cm) of snowfall. The Antarctic winter lasts from May through September. For several months during that time, Antarctica is in total darkness.

Icy winds make Antarctica feel even colder. Winds average 44 mph (70 km/h). Gusts along the coast often reach 120 mph (190 km/h). It's no wonder people call Antarctica the coldest, iciest, and windiest place on Earth.

Overview

Fill in the bubble to answer each question or complete each sentence.

1. The ____ divides East and West Antarctica.

   Ⓐ Antarctic Peninsula

   Ⓑ Southern Ocean

   Ⓒ Ross Sea

   Ⓓ Transantarctic Mountain Range

2. ____ is a large plateau region that is about 10,000 feet (3,000 m) above sea level.

   Ⓐ West Antarctica

   Ⓑ East Antarctica

   Ⓒ The Antarctic Peninsula

   Ⓓ An ice sheet

3. Which ocean is *not* part of the Southern Ocean?

   Ⓐ Arctic Ocean

   Ⓑ Indian Ocean

   Ⓒ Atlantic Ocean

   Ⓓ Pacific Ocean

4. Which statement is true about Antarctica's climate?

   Ⓐ Coastal Antarctica is colder than the interior.

   Ⓑ The Antarctic winter lasts from November through February.

   Ⓒ The Antarctic winter lasts from May through September.

   Ⓓ The interior of Antarctica gets much more snow than the coastal areas.

5. ____ fill bays and waterways along Antarctica's coasts.

   Ⓐ Peninsulas

   Ⓑ Glaciers

   Ⓒ Ice shelves

   Ⓓ Dry valleys

Formation of Antarctica

The hard outer layer of Earth's crust is made up of large sections called *tectonic plates.* The plates move very slowly over the surface of the Earth. As the plates move, they come together, move apart, or slide past each other. This continuous movement has been occurring for hundreds of millions of years, causing the continents to come together and split apart several times. The timeline below shows how Antarctica was formed the last time the continents separated.

About 300 Million Years Ago

All of the continents on Earth were joined together in a single supercontinent called *Pangaea.* Pangaea was surrounded by a global ocean called Panthalassa. Scientists believe the interior of the Pangaea supercontinent was a vast desert.

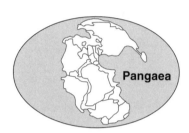

About 200 Million Years Ago

Pangaea broke apart. Two large landmasses were formed—*Laurasia* and *Gondwana.* Antarctica belonged to Gondwana, along with Africa, Australia, India, and South America. Antarctica was closer to the equator and was an ice-free land filled with plants and animals.

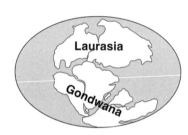

About 100 Million Years Ago

Gondwana and Laurasia broke up, and the seven landmasses began to shift in opposite directions. Antarctica broke away from Australia and South America, becoming a separate continent.

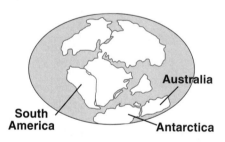

About 50 Million Years Ago

Antarctica drifted to the South Pole, and glaciers began to form. Other continents continued to drift farther apart, with great oceans separating the landmasses. India moved north and eventually joined the continent of Asia.

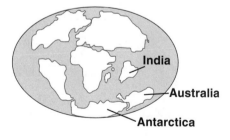

Present Day

In the current arrangement of the continents, Antarctica is still the farthest south. Ice has covered the continent for the last five million years.

The continents are still moving at the rate of an inch or more per year.

Formation of Antarctica

A. Read each statement. Unscramble the answer and write it on the line. Use the information on the other page to help you.

1. Earth once had a supercontinent called _____.

   gepaana

2. About 200 million years ago, Antarctica was part of _____.

   wodnagan

3. Antarctica was connected to South America and _____.

   suatraail

4. Africa, Antarctica, Australia, South America, and _____ were once part of Gondwana.

   inadi

5. About 100 million years ago, Antarctica became a separate

   _____.

   tincenont

6. _____ formed on Antarctica about 50 million years ago.

   lagceirs

7. Today, Antarctica is located at the _____.

   otush ople

8. Scientists have found fossils of plants and animals that lived on Antarctica

   when it was closer to the _____.

   eqtorua

B. Look at the drawing of Pangaea. Color the landmass that is present-day Antarctica.

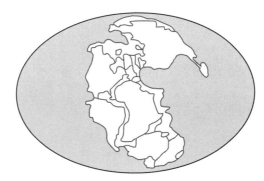

Antarctica's Harsh Landscape

Antarctica is situated around the southernmost point on Earth—the South Pole. About 98% of the continent is covered in ice and snow. Underneath the ice, Antarctica has mountains, lowlands, and valleys, just like any other continent. But high mountain peaks and bare rocky areas are the only visible landforms on Antarctica, other than ice. *Ice shelves*, which are extensions of thick ice sheets, stretch out into the ocean.

A. Look at the physical map of Antarctica on the other page. Use the map and key to fill in the blanks with the correct answers.

1. Which mountain range runs through the middle of the continent?   _____

2. What is the name of the major peak near the Ronne-Filchner Ice Shelf?   _____

3. What is the southernmost point on Earth called?   _____

4. What is the name of the mountain near the Ross Ice Shelf?   _____

5. What is the name of the large ice shelf above the Ellsworth Mountains?   _____

6. Which ice shelf juts out into the southern portion of the Indian Ocean?   _____

7. What is the name of the peninsula in West Antarctica?   _____

8. What is the name of the lowest point in Antarctica?   _____

B. Color the map on the other page according to the directions below.

1. Color the mountains brown.

2. Color the ice shelves gray.

3. Use red to circle the South Pole.

Name _____

Antarctica's Harsh Landscape

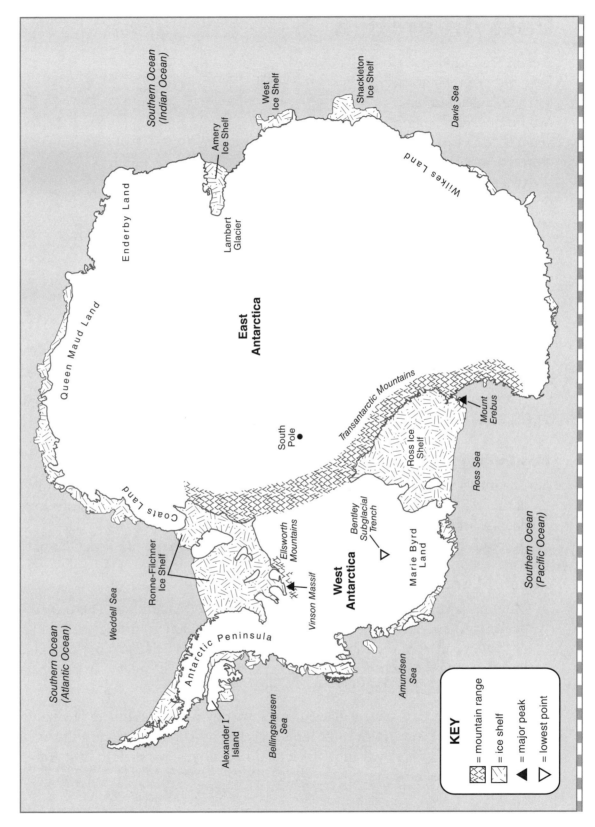

Southern Ocean
(Indian Ocean)

West
Ice Shelf

Shackleton
Ice Shelf

Davis Sea

Amery
Ice Shelf

Wilkes Land

Enderby Land

Lambert
Glacier

Queen Maud Land

East
Antarctica

Transantarctic Mountains

Mount
Erebus

South
Pole

Ross Ice
Shelf

Coats Land

Ross Sea

Bentley
Subglacial
Trench

Ellsworth
Mountains

Marie Byrd
Land

Southern Ocean
(Pacific Ocean)

Ronne-Filchner
Ice Shelf

West
Antarctica

Vinson Massif

Weddell Sea

Antarctic Peninsula

Amundsen
Sea

Alexander I
Island

Bellingshausen
Sea

Southern Ocean
(Atlantic Ocean)

KEY

= mountain range

= ice shelf

▲ = major peak

▷ = lowest point

East Antarctica

Antarctica is divided into East and West Antarctica by the Transantarctic Mountains. East Antarctica, also called Greater Antarctica, is the larger of the two regions. It makes up about two-thirds of the continent and contains the Geographic South Pole. The terrain in East Antarctica is so difficult that very few people travel to this area. In fact, this region is considered the most isolated place on Earth. It includes the areas of Coats Land, Enderby Land, Queen Maud Land, and Wilkes Land. These "lands" were named by explorers who discovered the areas.

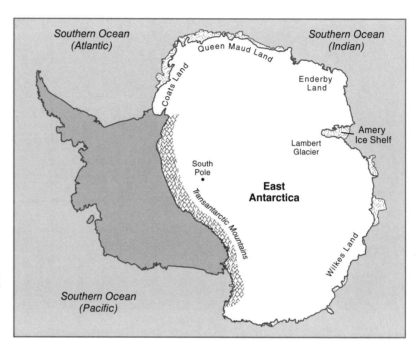

The Polar Plateau

The interior of East Antarctica is mostly an ice-capped plateau. The average thickness of the ice in East Antarctica is 7,303 feet (2,226 m). That's more than one mile (2.2 km) deep! Winds on the vast polar plateau blow snow into ridges up to 6 feet (1.8 m) high. Barren rock that is more than 570 million years old makes up about 2% of the plateau.

Coastal Landforms

Mountains run along much of the coastline of East Antarctica. There are 29 known peaks in this area whose summits are 6,562 feet (2,000 m) or higher. Small areas of dry valleys also dot the coastline. Tiny plants such as lichens, moss, and algae are found among the rocks in the dry valleys. However, the valleys have only a small amount of plant life since they are so cold and windy.

East Antarctica has several glaciers, or slow-moving bodies of ice. The Lambert Glacier in East Antarctica is the largest glacier in Antarctica and in the world. The Lambert Glacier is slowly moving north to the largest ice shelf in East Antarctica—the Amery Ice Shelf.

Name _____

East Antarctica

A. Read each statement. Circle **yes** if it is true or **no** if it is false. Use the information on the other page to help you.

1. East Antarctica is larger than West Antarctica.   **Yes**   **No**

2. Another name for East Antarctica is *Wilkes Land*.   **Yes**   **No**

3. East Antarctica is mostly a barren, rocky plain.   **Yes**   **No**

4. Enderby Land is on the coast of the Southern Ocean (Pacific).   **Yes**   **No**

5. The average thickness of the ice covering East Antarctica is   **Yes**   **No**
   more than one mile.

6. There are 29 peaks that are over 6,000 feet high in East Antarctica. **Yes**   **No**

7. Large amounts of lichens, moss, and algae live among the rocks   **Yes**   **No**
   in the dry valleys.

8. The Lambert Glacier is the largest glacier in the world.   **Yes**   **No**

9. The Lambert Glacier is slowly moving south.   **Yes**   **No**

10. Coats Land is near the Transantarctic Mountains.   **Yes**   **No**

B. Answer the questions using the information on the other page.

1. What is another name for East Antarctica?   _____

2. What is the name of the biggest ice shelf   _____
   in the region?

3. Which type of landform—mountain, plateau,   _____
   or valley—is most of East Antarctica?

4. Name three "lands" of East Antarctica.   _____

_____

West Antarctica

West Antarctica covers a much smaller area than East Antarctica. The region has a variety of landforms, including several record-breaking physical features.

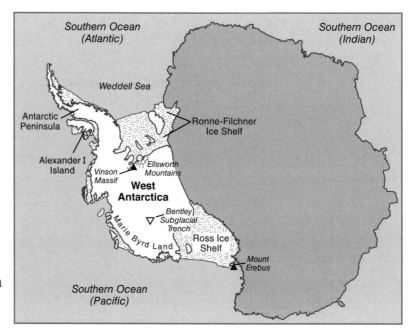

Elevation Features

The highest and lowest points on the continent are located on West Antarctica. The highest is Vinson Massif, a peak that stands in the Ellsworth Mountains. It is 16,049 feet (4,892 m) high and is located near the Antarctic Peninsula.

The lowest point is located in an area called the Bentley Subglacial Trench. It is 8,325 feet (2,555 m) below sea level. In fact, it is the lowest point on Earth that is not under water. However, the trench cannot be reached because it is buried under thick ice.

Another extreme feature in West Antarctica is Mount Erebus, located off the southeastern tip of the Ross Ice Shelf. It is Antarctica's most active volcano. The volcano stands 12,448 feet (3,794 m) high. Sometimes the volcano spurts out pieces of volcanic rock, and a lake of molten lava pools up in the inner crater of the mountain.

The Antarctic Peninsula

The Antarctic Peninsula is a mountainous, S-shaped piece of land that juts out to the northwest, toward South America. The peninsula has seven high mountain peaks that rise to 9,186 feet (2,800 m).

The coast of the peninsula has the mildest climate of anywhere in Antarctica. It is still bitterly cold, but tiny plants can grow on bare rocks there during the summer months.

There are also many islands along the peninsula. They are mostly covered in ice. The largest island is Alexander I Island.

Ice Shelves

There are five major ice shelves in West Antarctica. Four of them surround the Antarctic Peninsula. The largest of these is the Ronne-Filchner Ice Shelf. Farther south is the largest ice shelf on the continent and in the world—the Ross Ice Shelf.

West Antarctica

Read each clue below. Write the correct word on the numbered lines. Then use the numbers to crack the code!

1. Vinson Massif is the highest _____ in Antarctica.

$\overline{}\ \overline{}\ \overline{}\ \overline{}$
6 14 17 10

2. The lowest point in Antarctica is in the Bentley Subglacial _____.

$\overline{}\ \overline{}\ \overline{}\ \overline{}\ \overline{}\ \overline{}$
3 5 14 8 16 12

3. Mount Erebus is the most active _____ in Antarctica.

$\overline{}\ \overline{}\ \overline{}\ \overline{}\ \overline{}\ \overline{}\ \overline{}$
1 7 9 16 17 8 7

4. Alexander I _____ is off the coast of West Antarctica.

$\overline{}\ \overline{}\ \overline{}\ \overline{}\ \overline{}\ \overline{}$
11 4 9 17 8 15

5. The mountainous Antarctic _____ is surrounded by ice shelves.

$\overline{}\ \overline{}\ \overline{}\ \overline{}\ \overline{}\ \overline{}\ \overline{}\ \overline{}\ \overline{}$
6 14 8 11 8 4 2 9 17

6. The Ross _____ is the largest in Antarctica and in the world.

$\overline{}\ \overline{}\ \overline{}\quad\overline{}\ \overline{}\ \overline{}\ \overline{}\ \overline{}$
11 16 14   4 12 14 9 13

7. The _____ Mountains are located near the Ronne-Filchner Ice Shelf.

$\overline{}\ \overline{}\ \overline{}\ \overline{}\ \overline{}\ \overline{}\ \overline{}\ \overline{}\ \overline{}$
14 9 9 4 18 7 5 3 12

Crack the Code!

West Antarctica is sometimes called _____ Antarctica.

$\overline{}\ \overline{}\ \overline{}\ \overline{}\ \overline{}\ \overline{}$
9 14 4 4 14 5

Antarctic Mountains

Antarctica has a number of major mountain ranges, more than 1,500 mountain peaks, and at least two active volcanoes. Although many peaks are covered with ice and snow, some are bare. These bare peaks, called *nunataks*, rise starkly above the ice sheets.

The longest mountain system is the Transantarctic Mountain Range. It runs the length of the continent, from the Weddell Sea to the Ross Sea. This system, which is 1,243 miles (2,000 km) long, separates the two regions of East and West Antarctica. Four of the 10 highest mountains in Antarctica are found in the Transantarctic Mountains, near the Ross Ice Shelf.

On Ross Island, just off the Ross Ice Shelf, is Mount Erebus, the southernmost volcano on Earth. Mount Erebus was discovered in 1841 by explorer James Clark Ross and was named after one of his ships.

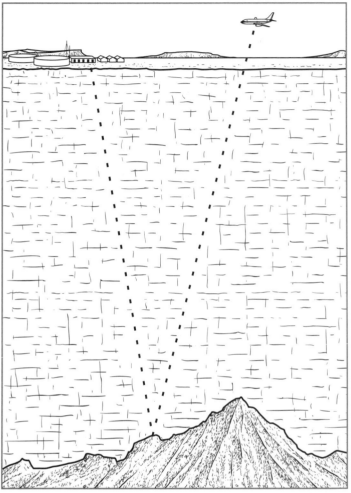

Scientists sent radar signals into thick sheets of ice to discover the Gamburtsev Mountains.

Farther north, another system that is about 990 miles (1,600 km) long covers most of the Antarctic Peninsula. At 10,446 feet (3,184 m), Mount Jackson is the highest peak there.

The five highest peaks on Antarctica, however, are in the Ellsworth Mountains, which run along the southern edge of the Ronne-Filchner Ice Shelf. These mountains contain the highest point on the continent—Vinson Massif, which is 16,049 feet (4,892 m) high. The peak was discovered by a U.S. Navy aircraft in 1958. It is named for Carl Vinson, a U.S. congressman who persuaded the government to support Antarctic exploration.

Perhaps the most interesting fact about the mountains of Antarctica is that many are buried under the ice. In fact, a huge subglacial mountain range called the Gamburtsev Mountains has been discovered about 2,000 feet below the ice in East Antarctica. Scientists used radar technology to map the mountains, which cover an area about the size of New York State. There are even lakes—liquid, not frozen—located in the mountains.

Antarctic Mountains

A. Circle the correct answer. Use the information on the other page to help you.

1. This peak is the highest in Antarctica.　　　　**Mount Jackson**　**Vinson Massif**

2. This is the longest mountain system.　　　　**Transantarctic**　**Ellsworth**

3. Four of the 10 tallest mountains are located on this landform.　　　　**Antarctic Peninsula**　**Transantarctic Mountains**

4. A navy airplane discovered this peak.　　　　**Mount Erebus**　**Vinson Massif**

5. These mountains have the five highest peaks on Antarctica.　　　　**Ellsworth**　**Gamburtsev**

6. This volcanic mountain is on Ross Island.　　　　**Vinson Massif**　**Mount Erebus**

7. This explorer discovered Mount Erebus.　　　　**Ross**　**Vinson**

8. These mountains are a subglacial range.　　　　**Gamburtsev**　**Transantarctic**

B. Use the information on the other page to answer the questions.

1. How were scientists able to know about mountains that are buried under the ice?

   _____

2. What is a nunatak?

   _____

3. What is a subglacial mountain range?

   _____

4. For whom is the highest peak in Antarctica named? Why?

   _____

   _____

Antarctic Ice

Ice Sheets

Nearly all of Antarctica is covered with two thick ice sheets, one on either side of the Transantarctic Mountains. Ice sheets are huge regions of ice formed from layers of snow pressed together over millions of years. The diagram below shows what Antarctica's surface would look like if you sliced it from northwest to southeast.

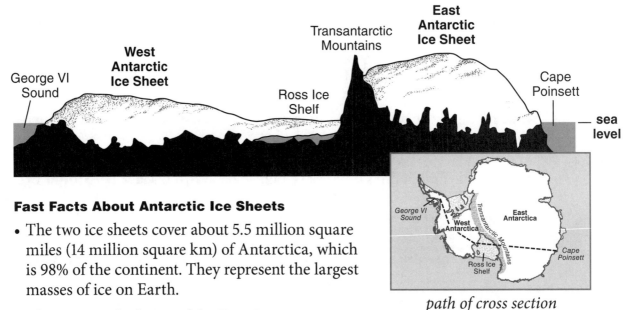

path of cross section

Fast Facts About Antarctic Ice Sheets

- The two ice sheets cover about 5.5 million square miles (14 million square km) of Antarctica, which is 98% of the continent. They represent the largest masses of ice on Earth.

- The average thickness of the East Antarctic ice sheet is 7,303 feet (2,226 m). The average thickness of the West Antarctic ice sheet is 4,285 feet (1,306 m).

- Together, the ice sheets contain about 7 million cubic miles (30 million cubic km) of ice. That is enough ice to carve a block the size of an Egyptian pyramid for every human on Earth!

- Antarctica's ice is so heavy that it has pushed the land in parts of the continent to below sea level. This weight also causes the ice to spread outward toward the coasts. Ice near the coasts moves as much as 660 feet (200 m) a year.

Glaciers

A glacier is a mass of slowly moving ice that was created by years of snowfall and cold temperatures. *Valley glaciers* are glaciers that flow through the valleys between mountains. The Lambert Glacier in East Antarctica is a valley glacier. It is about 60 miles (97 km) wide, over 250 miles (402 km) long, and about 1.5 miles (2.4 km) deep.

Together, the two enormous ice sheets in Antarctica are called a *continental glacier*. A continental glacier moves slowly outward from its center. The Antarctic continental glacier is flowing to the sea at a rate of about 3 to 33 feet (1 to 10 m) per year.

Antarctic Ice

Use the information and diagram about Antarctica's ice sheets on the other page to help you answer the questions below.

1. Which region—East or West Antarctica—has the thickest ice sheet? _____

2. What percentage of Antarctica is covered by ice sheets? _____

3. Which ice sheet has an average thickness of 4,285 feet (1,306 m)? _____

4. The diagram shows Antarctica from Cape Poinsett to which body of water? _____

5. Is the Ross Ice Shelf below, at, or above sea level? _____

6. How many cubic miles of ice are contained in the two ice sheets? _____

7. Does the weight of the ice sheets cause the ice to move toward the interior of the continent or to the coasts? _____

8. What is an ice sheet?

_____

9. How were the two Antarctic ice sheets formed?

_____

_____

10. Explain what a glacier is. Then explain what a valley glacier is.

_____

_____

_____

Antarctic Ice

Besides ice sheets and glaciers, Antarctica has other forms of ice. Ice shelves and icebergs are located along the edges of the continent, floating in the frigid waters off the coast.

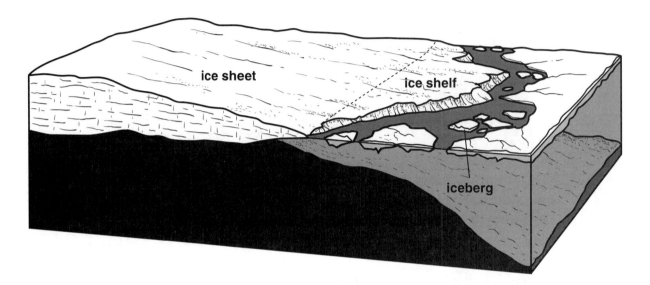

Ice Shelves

An ice shelf is a wide, thick platform of ice that floats on the water. An ice shelf forms where a glacier or ice sheet flows down to a coastline and extends onto the ocean surface. A total of 44% of the Antarctic coastline is covered with ice shelves. There are 43 named ice shelves in Antarctica, including the Ross Ice Shelf, which is the largest in Antarctica. It covers an area of 82,000 square miles (472,000 square km), about the size of the state of Idaho. The ice shelf is 500 miles (805 km) across, and its cliffs rise as high as 200 feet (61 m) above the sea.

Icebergs

An iceberg is a massive block of ice floating in the ocean. However, it is not frozen ocean water. It is a piece of freshwater ice that has broken off an ice shelf in a process called *calving*. Most Antarctic icebergs are *tabular icebergs*, which means they are flat-topped and square-cut. The ice often has a pale sky-blue or greenish tint, though only about one-seventh to one-fourth of an iceberg appears above the surface. The rest is below the water, creating a danger to passing ships.

The largest iceberg ever recorded in Antarctica was called B15. It calved off the Ross Ice Shelf in the year 2000. At 4,247 square miles (11,000 square km), it was nearly twice the size of the state of Delaware. About 120 feet (37 m) of the iceberg appeared above the surface, while 900 feet (274 m) of it was below the water. In 2002, B15 broke apart into smaller icebergs.

Antarctic Ice

A. Next to the ice-related term, write the letter of the clue that describes it. Use the information on the other page to help you.

_____ 1. calving

_____ 2. B15

_____ 3. tabular

_____ 4. iceberg

_____ 5. ice shelf

_____ 6. Ross Ice Shelf

a. a massive block of freshwater ice that floats in the ocean

b. the process of an iceberg breaking off an ice shelf

c. the largest ice shelf in Antarctica

d. the largest recorded iceberg

e. a type of iceberg that is flat-topped and square-cut

f. a wide, thick platform of ice that is located along the coastline

B. What is the difference between an ice shelf and an iceberg? Use the information on the other page to help you.

_____

_____

_____

C. Describe how part of an ice sheet can eventually become an iceberg. Use the information and diagram on the other page to help you.

_____

_____

_____

_____

Antarctica's Bodies of Water

The southern parts of the Atlantic, Indian, and Pacific oceans border Antarctica. These three oceans are collectively called the Southern Ocean.

Several seas that are part of the Southern Ocean also border the continent. They include the Amundsen, Bellingshausen, Davis, Ross, and Weddell seas. One of the largest bays is Prydz Bay along the eastern coast of Antarctica. A body of water called the McMurdo Sound is located on the eastern side of the Ross Sea. A *sound* is a long inlet of water that is generally parallel to the coastline.

There are no lakes on the surface of Antarctica. The only surface water is in the form of meltwater streams, or streams that flow from the melting of snow and ice in glacial areas. However, Antarctica does have a system of lakes and rivers beneath the surface of the ice sheets. Scientists have identified more than 145 of these subglacial lakes. The largest yet discovered is Lake Vostok. It has a surface area of roughly 5,400 square miles (14,000 square km), which is about the size of Lake Ontario. Some of the lakes are connected by rivers and streams that flow freely beneath the ice sheets.

A. Find and circle the names of the bodies of water in the word search. Words may appear across, down, or diagonally.

```
S  O  U  T  H  E  R  N  C  H  E  U  L  U  Q
A  E  G  J  N  A  I  B  A  R  L  O  Q  A  C
N  F  P  R  Y  D  Z  S  V  L  J  T  C  C  G
G  W  M  A  I  V  H  R  E  F  L  I  H  U  M
T  K  V  Z  T  N  H  D  R  I  F  O  D  Q  C
Z  A  A  U  G  S  D  N  D  I  I  F  U  F  M
E  M  V  L  W  E  I  A  C  L  W  L  Q  S  U
J  U  K  J  W  F  C  I  V  U  W  A  L  F  M
Y  N  K  E  Y  S  L  P  A  I  L  A  K  G  C
R  D  R  U  S  R  J  S  Y  H  S  F  T  N  M
V  S  W  O  V  O  S  T  O  K  G  K  C  A  U
N  E  R  E  A  R  S  C  A  E  K  F  A  G  R
K  N  V  I  V  O  S  K  O  T  L  G  A  X  D
D  K  T  S  N  G  A  O  L  H  J  Q  A  P  O
```

Ocean:
    Southern

Seas:
    Amundsen
    Davis
    Ross
    Weddell

Lake:
    Vostok

Bay/Sound:
    Prydz
    McMurdo

B. On the map on the other page, use blue to circle the names of the seas. Use red to circle the names of the bays. Use green to circle the names of the sounds and the cape.

Name _____

Physical Features

Antarctica's Bodies of Water

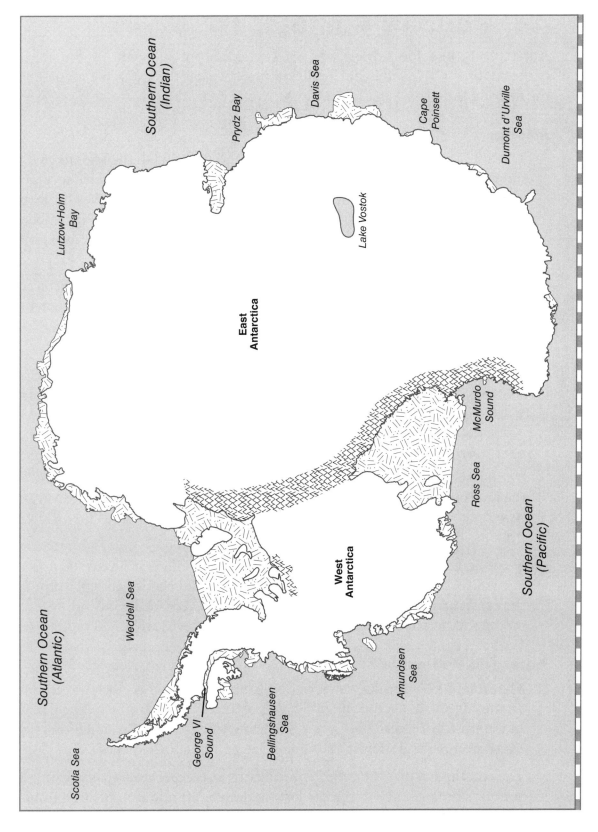

Southern Ocean (Indian)

Prydz Bay

Davis Sea

Cape Poinsett

Dumont d'Urville Sea

Lutzow-Holm Bay

Lake Vostok

East Antarctica

McMurdo Sound

Ross Sea

Southern Ocean (Pacific)

West Antarctica

Amundsen Sea

Southern Ocean (Atlantic)

Weddell Sea

Bellingshausen Sea

George VI Sound

Scotia Sea

Antarctica's Climate

Antarctica is the coldest, driest, and windiest continent on Earth. Yet different regions of the continent have different climates. Antarctica has three distinct climate regions—the interior, the coastal areas, and the Antarctic Peninsula.

Interior

The interior of the continent is the coldest and driest of all the regions. Average snowfall in the interior is less than 2 inches (5 cm) a year. There are several reasons why this region is so cold. Being closer to the South Pole, it receives the least light from the sun. In fact, during the winter months of May through September, Antarctica receives no sunlight at all. The interior also has a very high elevation, or height above sea level, which adds to the cold temperatures.

The average year-round temperature in the interior is –58°F (–50°C). The coldest recorded temperature was measured at –129°F (–89°C)! In the summer, which lasts from November through February, the temperatures warm up to an average of –22°F (–30°C).

The interior of Antarctica also experiences high winds. Violent gusts pick up drifting snow and cause blizzards. A severe blizzard may last for a week, with winds howling at 100 mph (161 km/h).

Coastal Areas

The coastal areas have more moderate temperatures and much more snowfall than the interior. Annual snowfall ranges from a total of 20 to 40 inches (51 to 102 cm). Average coastal winter temperatures range from 5° to 15°F (–10° to –15°C), but can drop to –58°F (–50°C).

Even though the coast is slightly warmer than the interior, the coastal areas still get icy winds. Cold winds that blow off the high central plateau and gain strength along the coasts are called *katabatic winds*. The highest recorded winds in Antarctica were on the southern coast of East Antarctica, where they reached 218 mph (351 km/h).

Antarctic Peninsula

The Antarctic Peninsula, being farther from the South Pole, has the mildest climate on the continent. Average monthly temperatures in the summer exceed 32°F (0°C). In the winter, temperatures rarely fall below 14°F (–10°C). Precipitation falls as rain in the summer and snow in the winter, averaging 14 to 20 inches (35 to 50 cm) a year.

The coastline of the Antarctic Peninsula can also experience strong winds and fierce storms. The gale-force winds can last for days or even weeks, creating rough seas along the peninsula.

Name _____

Antarctica's Climate

A. Circle the correct climate region of Antarctica. Use the information on the other page to help you.

1. The coldest temperature ever recorded was in this region.　　　**interior**　　　**peninsula**

2. The highest recorded winds were in this climate region.　　　**interior**　　　**coastal areas**

3. This region has the mildest climate.　　　**peninsula**　　　**coastal areas**

4. This climate region gets less than 2 inches of snow a year.　　　**coastal areas**　　　**interior**

5. In this region, yearly precipitation averages 14 to 20 inches.　　　**peninsula**　　　**coastal areas**

6. The lowest winter temperature can drop to –58°F in this region.　　　**interior**　　　**coastal areas**

7. In this climate region, rain falls in the summer and snow falls in the winter.　　　**coastal areas**　　　**peninsula**

8. Katabatic winds gain strength in this climate region.　　　**coastal areas**　　　**interior**

9. The annual snowfall in this region ranges from 51 to 102 cm.　　　**interior**　　　**coastal areas**

10. The elevation of this climate region is high.　　　**peninsula**　　　**interior**

B. In which climate region of Antarctica do you think it would be easiest for people to live? Explain your answer.

_____

_____

Climate Changes in Antarctica

Many scientists around the globe are concerned that parts of Antarctica are warming up. Researchers have also learned that the ozone layer over Antarctica is getting thinner. Both of these factors could affect the future of the icy continent of Antarctica and of the world.

Warming in Antarctica

Over the past 50 years, the west coast of the Antarctic Peninsula has been one of the most rapidly warming areas on Earth. Average annual temperatures have risen by nearly 5.5°F (3°C).

Many glaciers and about 10 ice shelves that border the Antarctic Peninsula have retreated, or shrunk in size, in recent years. Some have collapsed completely. For example, the Larsen Ice Shelf along the coast of the Antarctic Peninsula is falling apart. One part of the ice shelf collapsed in 1995. A second part collapsed in 2002. The remaining section of the ice shelf appears to be stable, but some scientists predict that if warming continues at its current rate, it could also fall.

Warming of the Southern Ocean has also been observed. Ocean temperatures to the west of the Antarctic Peninsula have increased by nearly 2°F (1°C) since 1955.

As the temperatures rise in Antarctica, more and more ice melts away. If the ice continues to melt at such a fast rate, ocean levels could rise, endangering many coastal cities around the world.

The Antarctic Ozone Hole

The ozone layer is a layer of ozone gas, a form of oxygen, that is part of Earth's atmosphere. The ozone layer protects Earth and its living things from dangerous ultraviolet radiation in the sun's rays. In 1985, scientists discovered that there was a hole in the ozone layer over Antarctica. The hole is not really a hole, but a large area with extremely low levels of ozone gas. The low levels usually appear around September and then return to normal by December. Scientists concluded that pollution from synthetic chemicals was causing the ozone to become thinner. Synthetic chemicals are used in cleaning products, cooling fluid in refrigerators, and aerosol sprays.

In 2006, scientists at NASA (National Aeronautics and Space Administration) discovered that the ozone hole was the largest it had ever been, covering 10 million square miles (27 million square km). Since then, the hole has become slightly smaller in size and the ozone levels have increased, though they are still far below what they were 30 years ago. Despite this short-term improvement, many scientists still fear that the ozone hole could cause damage to the ice, fish, and marine plants in Antarctica.

Climate Changes in Antarctica

A. Use the information on the other page to answer the questions.

1. Which part of Antarctica is the most
   rapidly warming region?   _____

2. How many ice shelves along the Antarctic
   Peninsula have retreated?   _____

3. Which ice shelf has had two parts collapse?   _____

4. Which ocean has seen increases in temperature
   of nearly 2°F since 1955?   _____

5. What is the ozone layer?

   _____

6. What does the ozone layer do?

   _____

7. During what months does the ozone hole appear over Antarctica?

   _____

8. What do scientists think is the cause of the ozone hole?

   _____

B. What effects could warming in Antarctica and a decrease in ozone levels have on
Antarctica and the world?

_____

_____

_____

Review

Use words from the box to complete the crossword puzzle.

continent

Lambert

Mountains

Pangaea

peak

Ross

sheets

Southern

Trench

Across

1. The Bentley Subglacial ____ is the lowest point in Antarctica.

4. The ____ Ocean surrounds the continent.

7. The ____ Glacier is the largest in Antarctica and in the world.

8. The ____ Ice Shelf is the largest in Antarctica.

9. The highest ____ in Antarctica is called Vinson Massif.

Down

2. Antarctica is the coldest, highest, and windiest ____ in the world.

3. The Transantarctic ____ form a natural border between East and West Antarctica.

5. Two immense ice ____ cover 98% of the continent.

6. All of Earth's continents were once part of a huge landmass called ____.

History of Exploration

This section introduces students to three different historical periods of Antarctic exploration. Students learn how early explorers braved the icy waters to discover lands along the Antarctic coast. Students also read about the exploits of explorers who searched for a way to the South Pole during the Heroic Age. Lastly, students find out about the men who explored the continent by air.

Each skill in this section is based on the following National Geography Standards:

Essential Element 5: Environment and Society

Standard 7: How physical systems affect human systems

Essential Element 6: The Uses of Geography

Standard 17: How to apply geography to interpret the past

CONTENTS

Overview

Antarctica was the last of the seven continents to be explored. It was difficult to reach because it was remote and surrounded by stormy, icy waters. Brave explorers took their chances to become the first to discover new areas of this "unknown southern land."

Early Exploration

Early explorers of Antarctica sailed south into icy waters and traveled along the continent's coast. No one knows for certain which explorer was the first to see Antarctica. But all agree that in 1773, British sea captain James Cook was the first to sail across the *Antarctic Circle*, the latitude line that lies almost 67° south of the equator and marks Antarctic territory. Later, in 1820, Russian explorer Fabian von Bellingshausen was credited for sighting land.

Other explorers soon followed. In 1823, James Weddell sailed farther south than anyone before him. Charles Wilkes mapped the eastern coastline of the icy continent in 1840. Explorer James Clark Ross explored the southernmost point of the Antarctic coast two years later. And in the late 1820s, Commander Adrien de Gerlache and his crew became the first to survive a treacherous winter aboard their ship in frozen Antarctic waters.

The Heroic Age

The early 1900s were called the "Heroic Age" of exploration. During this period, explorers charted unknown inland territories. Four explorers stand out from this era. Douglas Mawson and Ernest Shackleton each led three expeditions into the interior of the continent. Both survived a dangerous second expedition. Roald Amundsen and Robert Falcon Scott raced to be the first to the South Pole. Many times during their journeys, the men had to ski or trudge through blizzards, total darkness, and below-freezing temperatures.

Exploration by Air

In 1928, Australian explorer George Hubert Wilkins was the first to make a short flight into the Antarctic region. After that first flight, Americans dominated air exploration. American Richard E. Byrd was the first to fly over the South Pole. Later, Lincoln Ellsworth crossed the continent by air.

Then, in 1947, the U.S. Navy launched large expeditions to Antarctica to set up bases and conduct scientific research. They used newer airplanes and helicopters and worked to produce accurate maps of the continent. From that time on, many nations from around the world joined in the scientific exploration of Antarctica.

Overview

Fill in the bubble to answer each question or complete each sentence.

1. Antarctica was the _____ of the seven continents to be explored.

   Ⓐ first

   Ⓑ last

   Ⓒ third

   Ⓓ sixth

2. _____ was the first explorer to cross the Antarctic Circle.

   Ⓐ James Cook

   Ⓑ James Clark Ross

   Ⓒ Ernest Shackleton

   Ⓓ Roald Amundsen

3. Which two explorers competed in a race to be the first to the South Pole?

   Ⓐ Ross and Wilkes

   Ⓑ Wilkins and Byrd

   Ⓒ Amundsen and Scott

   Ⓓ Mawson and Shackleton

4. Which statement about Antarctic exploration is true?

   Ⓐ Explorers during the Heroic Age led expeditions into the interior of Antarctica.

   Ⓑ During the 1700s, early explorers traveled on land to the South Pole.

   Ⓒ Explorers flew their planes over the Antarctic continent in the 1800s.

   Ⓓ During the Heroic Age, explorers used airplanes to map the coast of Antarctica.

5. Which country led the way in exploration by air from 1929 to the 1940s?

   Ⓐ England

   Ⓑ Russia

   Ⓒ Australia

   Ⓓ the United States

Unknown Southern Land

Two thousand years ago, before the continent of Antarctica was actually discovered, great thinkers believed a large southern land existed. Ancient Greek philosophers thought that there had to be a landmass at Earth's southern end to balance the weight of the lands in the north.

Naming the Continent

During the second century AD, Roman geographer and astronomer Ptolemy called the possible landmass *Terra Australis Incognita*, which means "unknown southern land" in Latin. Ptolemy believed the land was inhabited and had rich soil. The name *Antarctica* later came from two Greek words meaning "opposite the Bear." The Bear is a constellation of stars seen from the northernmost region of Earth.

European Exploration

It was centuries before anyone attempted to prove that a southern continent existed. Starting in the 1400s, European explorers began to sail south. In 1520, Ferdinand Magellan found a narrow passage at the tip of South America connecting the Atlantic and Pacific oceans. There was land to the south of the passage, and geographers thought it might be the edge of a southern continent. But it turned out to be a group of islands at the southern tip of South America.

As other European explorers used the narrow passage called the Strait of Magellan to reach the Pacific Ocean, many were blown south by ferocious storms. These sailors discovered more and more islands. However, none saw the immense landmass of Antarctica.

Captain Cook's Voyages

Despite not being able to find the landmass, people still believed Antarctica existed. In 1768, British captain James Cook set sail in search of the continent. Cook didn't find Antarctica, but he did end up exploring New Zealand.

In 1773, Cook led another expedition south and became the first explorer to cross the Antarctic Circle. Cook's ships encountered harsh storms, thick fogs, and large icebergs in the Southern Ocean. Cook thought that the icebergs could only be caused by thick ice that came from a landmass. When Cook got back to England, he reported that even if there was land, a place that had such terrible storms, bitterly cold winds, and large amounts of ice was not fit for human settlement.

Scientists now know that Captain Cook was about 70 miles (113 km) north of the Antarctic coast. It would be nearly 50 years until any other explorer would dare to follow Cook's path south and set foot on the frozen southern continent.

Unknown Southern Land

Use the information on the other page to help you answer the questions below.

1. What does *Terra Australis Incognita* mean?   _____

2. Which explorer found a passage between the   _____
   Atlantic and Pacific oceans?

3. In what year did Captain James Cook cross the   _____
   Antarctic Circle?

4. What landmass did Captain Cook find before he   _____
   crossed the Antarctic Circle?

5. Scientists know that Captain Cook came within   _____
   how many miles of the Antarctic landmass?

6. What does the name *Antarctica* mean in Greek?

   _____

7. What did Ptolemy wrongly guess about Antarctica?

   _____

8. What did Captain Cook correctly conclude about icebergs in the Southern Ocean?

   _____

   _____

9. Why didn't Captain Cook believe that Antarctica could be settled by humans?

   _____

   _____

   _____

Early Exploration

In the 1800s, explorers from Europe and the United States sailed into the Southern Ocean looking for the riches of the unknown continent. Some were naval officers trying to claim lands for their countries. Some were sea captains hunting seals and whales. Others were scientists looking for new discoveries. They all became geographers, mapping the coastline of the immense continent of Antarctica.

Below is a timeline of some of the important events of the 1800s.

1820   Russian captain Fabian von Bellingshausen is the first person to see the Antarctic Peninsula.

1821   American seal hunter John Davis and his crew are the first people to set foot on the Antarctic continent.

1823   British seal hunter James Weddell sails farther south than any previous explorer. He finds what is now called the Weddell Sea.

1838   French lieutenant Jules Dumont d'Urville explores the East Antarctic coastline. He names both the land and the penguins that live there after his wife, Adélie.

1840   American naval officer Charles Wilkes proves that Antarctica is a continent by sailing more than 1,500 miles (2,400 km) along the coast of the landmass.

1842   British explorer James Clark Ross reaches the southernmost point of Antarctica. He discovers the Ross Ice Shelf, Victoria Land, and Mount Erebus, an active volcano.

1898   Belgian commander Adrien de Gerlache and his crew are the first to survive an Antarctic winter when their ship becomes trapped in *pack ice*, or seawater that has an icy crust, off the Antarctic Peninsula.

1899   Norwegian explorer Carsten Borchgrevink and his crew are the first to build huts and spend a winter on the continent.

Early Exploration

A. Read each statement. Circle **yes** if it is true or **no** if it is false. Use the information on the other page to help you.

1. Most early exploration took place between 1800 and 1821.　　　**Yes**　　No

2. Captain von Bellingshausen was the first to set foot on Antarctic land.　　　**Yes**　　No

3. James Weddell found the Weddell Sea in 1823.　　　**Yes**　　No

4. Mount Erebus, an active volcano, was discovered by James Clark Ross.　　　**Yes**　　No

5. French lieutenant Dumont d'Urville discovered both Adélie Land and Victoria Land.　　　**Yes**　　No

6. Charles Wilkes sailed more than 1,500 miles along the Antarctic coast.　　　**Yes**　　No

7. In 1840, Lieutenant Adrien de Gerlache and his crew became trapped in pack ice off the Antarctic Peninsula.　　　**Yes**　　No

8. No human spent a winter on the harsh continent before 1899.　　　**Yes**　　No

9. The first person to see the Antarctic Peninsula was from Russia.　　　**Yes**　　No

10. All the explorers contributed to mapping the coastline of Antarctica.　　　**Yes**　　No

B. List three reasons that explorers sailed to Antarctica in the 1800s. Use the information on the other page to help you.

_____

_____

_____

Early Exploration

Fabian von Bellingshausen
Antarctic Exploration 1819–1821

James Weddell
Antarctic Exploration 1822–1824

- Captain Bellingshausen was chosen by the Russian navy to command an expedition to Antarctica. In 1819, nearly 200 officers and crew members boarded two ships and set sail. Their mission was to get as close as possible to the unknown southern land.

- On January 26, 1820, Bellingshausen crossed the Antarctic Circle. The next day, he came within 20 miles (32 km) of the Antarctic Peninsula and most likely saw it from his ship.

- On January 21, 1821, Bellingshausen saw islands inside the Antarctic Circle off the coast of the Antarctic Peninsula. He named them Peter I Island and Alexander I Island. They are in what is now called the Bellingshausen Sea.

- Bellingshausen sailed home, satisfied that he had claimed lands for Russia. His voyage lasted nearly two years.

- Weddell left the British navy to sail commercial ships. Seal skins were highly valued at the time, and Weddell intended to hunt seals. He bought two small seal-hunting ships and hired a crew of 35.

- In 1822, Weddell set sail for Antarctic waters, where he knew the ocean was teeming with seals.

- In January of 1823, Weddell sailed near the South Orkney Islands, just north of the Antarctic Peninsula. There, he found a new kind of seal that was later named the Weddell seal.

- In February of 1823, Weddell sailed farther south than any explorer before him. He discovered a great body of water that he called George IV Sea. It was later renamed the Weddell Sea.

- Weddell returned to England and wrote about his journey in the book called *A Voyage Towards the South Pole*.

Early Exploration

A. Read each question. Fill in the correct answer for each explorer. Use the information on the other page to help you.

1. What was each explorer's mission?

   Bellingshausen: _____

   Weddell: _____

2. What did each explorer discover?

   Bellingshausen: _____

   _____

   Weddell: _____

   _____

B. Look at the map of the Antarctic Peninsula and the seas and islands that are near it. Use yellow to circle the names of the lands and seas that Bellingshausen saw. Then use green to circle the names of the lands and seas that Weddell saw.

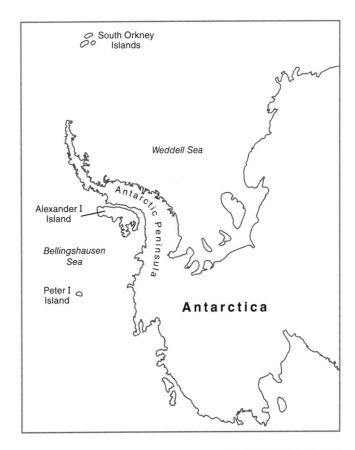

Early Exploration

Charles Wilkes
Antarctic Exploration 1838–1840

James Clark Ross
Antarctic Exploration 1839–1843

- In 1838, at the direction of the American navy, Charles Wilkes led 433 men on a scientific expedition to the Antarctic. Seven scientists and two artists went along to study and record the plants, animals, rocks, minerals, and landforms of Antarctica.

- In 1840, lookouts on three ships spotted land on the southeastern side of Antarctica. The ships tried to get closer, but huge *ice floes* (floating chunks of ice) and an ice shelf stopped them.

- Wilkes was able to map more than 1,500 miles (2,400 km) of the eastern coastline. This distance showed that Antarctica was large enough to be a continent.

- Wilkes returned to the U.S. and wrote five volumes about his expedition. Many years later, Wilkes was recognized for his discoveries. Wilkes Land in East Antarctica was named in his honor.

- In 1839, British navy captain James Clark Ross and 134 men set sail hoping to go farther south than any before them. Ross's intention was to find the Magnetic South Pole, which, like the Magnetic North Pole, is where Earth's magnetic field is strongest. The magnetic poles are located close to the geographic poles.

- In 1841, Ross discovered what is now called the Ross Sea and Victoria Land. He also discovered two volcanoes, which he named Mount Erebus and Mount Terror, after his ships. In addition, he sailed along the edge of what was later named the Ross Ice Shelf.

- After spending the winter in Tasmania, Australia, Ross returned to Antarctica. In 1842, he sailed farther south than anyone had ever been. His record stood until 1900.

- Ross returned to England and was knighted for his bravery and his discoveries. Nonetheless, he was disappointed that he had not located the Magnetic South Pole.

Name _____

Early Exploration

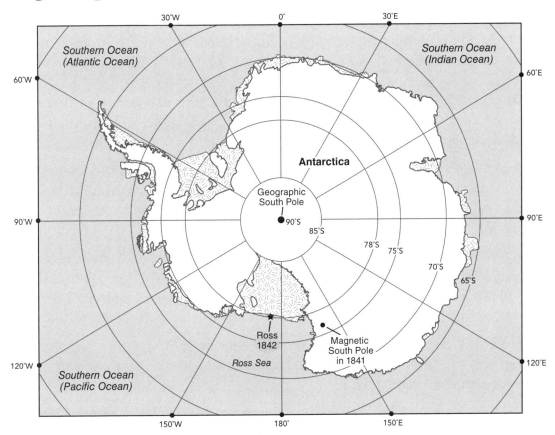

On January 23, 1842, James Clark Ross reached a point farther south than anyone before him had been. "Farthest south" in this case refers to the southernmost latitude reached by an explorer. Ross's latitude reading was about 78°S when he was in the Ross Sea. The Geographic South Pole, the southernmost point on the planet, is at 90°S latitude. The Magnetic South Pole, which changes position slightly over time, was in East Antarctica at about 76°S latitude then.

Write two questions that can be answered using information from the map and caption. Then answer the questions.

1. _____

   _____

2. _____

   _____

Voyage of the *Belgica*

The journey of the ship *Belgica,* under the command of Adrien de Gerlache, was supposed to be a purely scientific expedition. But because of a variety of problems, the voyage became one of survival—and one of the most harrowing tales in Antarctic history.

August 16, 1897: Commander de Gerlache sets sail from Belgium in a ship called the *Belgica.* Among his crew of 19 are a chief scientist, a geologist, and a young first mate named Roald Amundsen.

December 1897: Commander de Gerlache decides to explore Tierra del Fuego, a group of islands at the tip of South America. Other officers warn him that the end of the polar summer is approaching, which means bad weather will come soon. He pays no attention and orders the ship to cruise the islands anyway.

January 1898: The *Belgica* arrives in Antarctic waters. A strong storm hits, and Karl Wiencke, a sailor, falls into the ocean and is lost. For a month, the scientists study and name 20 islands along a waterway that was later named Gerlache Strait. They take some of the first photographs of Antarctica.

March 1898: When the ship crosses the Antarctic Circle, it hits thick pack ice and becomes lodged. Amundsen writes that they are stuck in the Antarctic without winter clothes or adequate provisions.

May 1898: The crew will not see daylight again for 70 days. Food becomes scarce. Crew members come down with *scurvy,* a disease caused by malnutrition. The commander refuses to let the men eat fresh penguin meat, but Frederick Cook, the ship's doctor, insists. He orders the men to eat penguin, and they soon recover.

October 1898: The crew cheers when they see pools of water forming in the ice. But then the ice closes in and freezes again. Soon, the men begin to run short of coal and oil. Panic sets in, and several crew members have to be treated for depression. On moonlit nights, they go skiing on the ice to relieve their boredom.

December 1898: On New Year's Eve, the crew sees open water 2,100 feet (640 m) away. Cook suggests cutting a passage through the ice by hand. The men work day and night, and by the end of January, they have hacked through over 2,000 feet (600 m) of ice. But a few days later, the pressure from the surrounding ice closes up their passage.

March 1899: On February 15, the passage they had cut reopens and extends right up to the ship. The crew slowly inches the *Belgica* forward. By March 14, they have cut through 7 miles (11 km) of ice to the open sea. They are on their way home!

November 5, 1899: The *Belgica* sails back to Belgium safely. The expedition has gathered valuable scientific data. Despite his many mistakes, Commander de Gerlache is given a hero's welcome.

Voyage of the *Belgica*

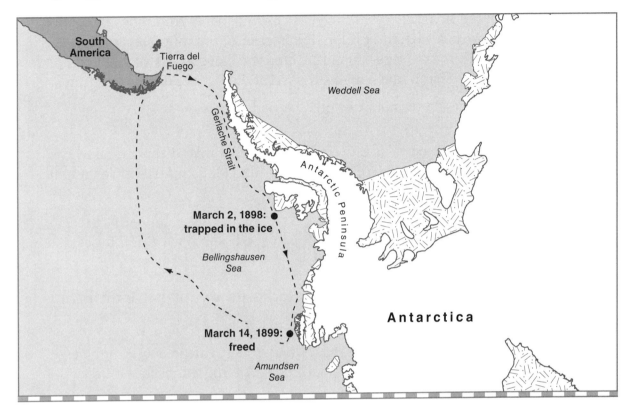

Write the letter of the voyage event that matches each month and year.

_____ 1. August 1897

_____ 2. January 1898

_____ 3. December 1897

_____ 4. March 1898

_____ 5. May 1898

_____ 6. March 1899

_____ 7. October 1898

_____ 8. December 1898

_____ 9. November 1899

a. The crew of the *Belgica* returns to Belgium.

b. A sailor falls to his death into the sea.

c. The crew sees open water on New Year's Eve.

d. The *Belgica* is freed from the ice and sails into the open sea.

e. Commander de Gerlache sets sail from Belgium on his voyage to Antarctica.

f. The crew explores Tierra del Fuego.

g. Pools of water form in the ice, but they soon freeze up again.

h. Total darkness sets in for 70 days and nights.

i. The *Belgica* becomes lodged in pack ice.

The Heroic Age

The first 20 years of the 1900s are often called the Heroic Age of Antarctic exploration. During this period, the goals were to explore the interior of the continent and to reach the South Pole. Four explorers—Roald Amundsen, Douglas Mawson, Robert Falcon Scott, and Ernest Shackleton—made important discoveries during this time.

Below is a timeline of the four famous explorers' expeditions.

1901 British explorer Robert Falcon Scott leads the first inland expedition to Antarctica. He travels to within about 520 miles (840 km) of the Geographic South Pole.

1907 Irish explorer Ernest Shackleton leads an expedition to within 97 miles (180 km) of the Geographic South Pole.

1909 Australian explorer Douglas Mawson reaches the area of the Magnetic South Pole.

1911 Norwegian explorer Roald Amundsen and Robert Falcon Scott compete to be the first to the Geographic South Pole. Amundsen reaches it first on December 14.

1911 Douglas Mawson leads his second expedition into the interior. In January, he discovers an area of land on the southeastern tip of Antarctica that he names George V Land.

1912 Robert Falcon Scott becomes the second person to reach the Geographic South Pole on January 17.

1914 Ernest Shackleton leads his second expedition, hoping to cross the continent. However, his ship, the *Endurance,* is crushed by ice, and he and his crew must fight to survive. After several months, they finally return home.

1921 Ernest Shackleton leads his third expedition to Antarctica. He dies on board his ship in January 1922 at South Georgia Island, north of the Antarctic Peninsula. Shackleton's death brings the Heroic Age of Antarctic exploration to a close.

The Heroic Age

A. Circle the correct explorer. Use the information on the other page to help you.

1. Robert Falcon Scott and this explorer raced to be the first to reach the Geographic South Pole.

   Amundsen **Mawson**

2. On his second voyage, this explorer's ship was crushed by ice.

   Scott **Shackleton**

3. This explorer reached the area of the Magnetic South Pole.

   Mawson **Amundsen**

4. This explorer was the second person to reach the Geographic South Pole.

   Scott **Amundsen**

5. In 1901, this explorer led the first journey to the interior of Antarctica.

   Shackleton **Scott**

6. This explorer discovered George V Land.

   Mawson **Shackleton**

7. This explorer reached the Geographic South Pole on December 14, 1911.

   Amundsen **Scott**

8. This explorer's death marked the end of the Heroic Age of Antarctic exploration.

   Shackleton **Amundsen**

B. What personal characteristics do you think it would take to be an Antarctic explorer? Name at least two and explain why you think they are important.

_____

_____

_____

_____

The Heroic Age

Ernest Shackleton
Antarctic Exploration 1907–1922

Douglas Mawson
Antarctic Exploration 1907–1931

- In 1907, Ernest Shackleton led his first Antarctic expedition to within 97 miles (180 km) of the Geographic South Pole.

- Shackleton's second expedition was a perilous journey that lasted from 1914 to 1917. He and his crew sailed into the Weddell Sea, where ice crushed and sank his ship. For five months, Shackleton and the crew camped out on the ice. They escaped in lifeboats to Elephant Island, but found that it was deserted.

  Shackleton and five other men journeyed north by boat to South Georgia Island looking for help. They had to hike for 36 hours over the island's glacier-covered land to reach a small town. Fishermen helped Shackleton get a boat for the trip back to Elephant Island. After three months of sailing, he and his five men rescued the rest of the crew. Not a single person died during the expedition.

- Shackleton undertook a third expedition in 1921. Sadly, his mission of sailing around Antarctica was cut short when he died of a heart attack on the ship.

- Douglas Mawson's first expedition was in 1907, when he joined Shackleton's expedition as a scientist. In 1908, he reached the summit of Mount Erebus, Antarctica's most active volcano.

- In 1909, Mawson was in the expedition party that was the first to reach the Magnetic South Pole.

- Mawson's next expedition, which lasted from 1911 to 1914, was a harrowing experience. During his travels, one companion fell into a *crevasse,* or deep crack in the ice, and died, taking most of the supplies with him. Mawson and another crew member, Xavier Mertz, had to kill and eat their sled dogs to survive. Mertz fell ill from eating the dogs' livers and died. After hauling himself out of another crevasse, Mawson returned to base to discover that his ship, the *Aurora,* had left without him. He and six companions had to wait an entire year before the ship came back.

- Mawson returned to Antarctica in 1929. This trip led to Australia claiming 42% of Antarctica.

The Heroic Age

A. Write the name of the explorer—Shackleton or Mawson—described in each clue. Use the information on the other page to help you.

1. This explorer pulled himself out of a crevasse.   _____

2. This explorer's ship was crushed by ice.   _____

3. This explorer rescued his crew without losing one life.   _____

4. This explorer was the leader of an expedition in 1907.   _____

5. This explorer was stranded for a year until his ship returned to Antarctica.   _____

6. This explorer claimed land for Australia.   _____

7. This explorer camped out on sea ice for five months.   _____

8. This explorer was the first to reach the Magnetic South Pole.   _____

9. This explorer's companion died from eating the livers of his sled dogs.   _____

10. This explorer journeyed to South Georgia Island.   _____

B. Do you think that Ernest Shackleton and Douglas Mawson were both brave men? Explain your answer.

_____

_____

_____

Race to the South Pole

During the Heroic Age, reaching the geographic South Pole was one of the main goals of explorers. In 1911, two groups of men led by Roald Amundsen and Robert Falcon Scott found themselves in a race to be the first to reach the South Pole. Their approaches to the challenge were very different, and only one explorer returned to tell of his journey.

Amundsen's Ship: the *Fram*
Crew: 19 men
Animals: 97 dogs
Equipment: sledges (sleds for hauling supplies), skis, a portable hut, and tents

Scott's Ship: the *Terra Nova*
Crew: 65 men
Animals: 33 dogs, 19 ponies
Equipment: sledges, two experimental motorized sledges, and skis

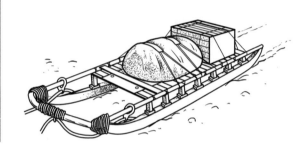

Amundsen's and Scott's Routes to the South Pole

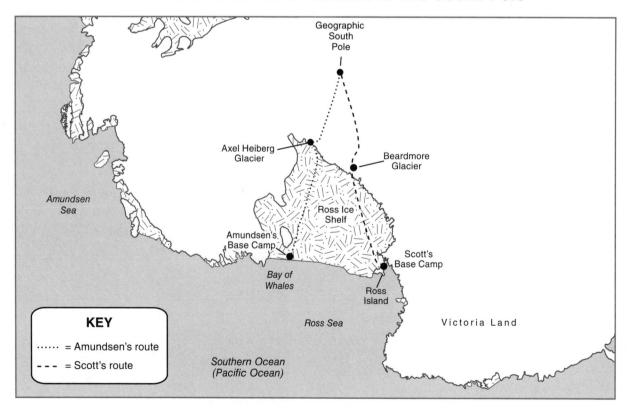

Race to the South Pole

Roald Amundsen's Expedition

Roald Amundsen

August 9, 1910: The *Fram* leaves Norway.

January 14, 1911: The *Fram* reaches the Bay of Whales off the Ross Ice Shelf. Base camp is set up two miles inland. For the next three weeks, five sledges, 46 dogs, and five men transfer tons of supplies from the ship to the camp. The hut where the men will live is built, and a storage area for equipment is created.

February 1911: *Depots*, or stopping points along the route to the South Pole, are established. Supplies are buried under piles of rocks called *cairns* at each stop.

April 1911: The crew returns to base camp to wait during the next four months of total darkness. Throughout the long winter, the men make scientific observations, repair and pack the sledges with food, and make new tents for the long journey.

September 1911: Eight men with sledges pulled by 86 dogs head out. They cover 31 miles (50 km) over the next three days. Then the temperature drops to –70°F (–57°C). The team heads back to base camp for fear that all the dogs will freeze to death.

October 20, 1911: Amundsen and four men—Olav Bjaaland, Helmer Hanssen, Sverre Hassel, and Oscar Wisting—depart for the South Pole. Four sledges are used, each pulled by 13 dogs. Four days later they arrive at a cairn. They uncover provisions and feed the dogs seal meat and blubber. The next day the party leaves with all five men on skis. The dogs pull the loaded sledges.

November 1911: The party arrives at Queen Maud's Range, and the men realize they are 340 miles (547 km) from the pole. They climb up a glacier to an elevation of 10,000 feet (3,048 m). Twenty-four dogs have to be killed because they are too sick to go on. For the next 10 days, the five men and the remaining 28 dogs struggle through a raging blizzard. Unfortunately, more dogs are lost.

December 14, 1911: The men are frostbitten, and the remaining 16 dogs are exhausted, but they push on. At 3:00 p.m., all the men shout "Halt!" Their instruments register a latitude of 90°S. They have made it to the Geographic South Pole. The men plant the Norwegian flag and put up a tent. Amundsen leaves a message inside for Robert Scott, along with a letter for the king of Norway proving the accomplishment.

January 1912: The return trip takes 39 days. The party returns with all five men and the dogs. The *Fram* is waiting in the bay to take the heroes back home.

March 7, 1912: From Hobart, Tasmania, Amundsen sends a cable to his brother with the historic news. The world would soon know that Norwegian explorer Roald Amundsen was the first person to reach the South Pole.

Race to the South Pole

Robert Falcon Scott's Expedition

Robert Falcon Scott

June 1, 1910: The *Terra Nova* leaves the United Kingdom.

January 4, 1911: The *Terra Nova* reaches McMurdo Sound off the eastern side of the Ross Ice Shelf. Base camp is set up at Cape Evans, just west of Ross Island. Motorized sledges are used to carry supplies from the ship to base camp. A hut is constructed. Sixteen officers and nine crewmen stay at camp.

November 1, 1911: Sixteen men, 10 ponies, and 23 dogs start out for the pole with motorized sledges. The sledges soon fail, and the ponies struggle.

December 1911: A blizzard hits, and five ponies die. The men press on to the Beardmore Glacier. Each man has to haul a sledge up and over the 10,000-foot (3,048-m) glacier, pulling more than 200 pounds (91 kg) through the snow and ice.

January 3, 1912: Scott chooses four men—Henry Bowers, Edgar Evans, Lawrence Oates, and Edward Wilson—to continue with him to the South Pole. The other exhausted men return to base camp. By January 10, Scott's party has traveled to within about 97 miles (156 km) of the pole.

January 17, 1912: Scott and his frostbitten men reach the South Pole only to see the Norwegian flag blowing in the wind. Scott writes, "Well, we have turned our back now on the goal of our ambition with sore feelings... Goodbye to the daydreams!"

February 1912: Scott and his men trudge through blizzard conditions to reach the depot near Beardmore Glacier on their way back from the pole. They are all badly frostbitten. The men reduce their rations since there are long distances between each depot stop. Evans has to be carried by sledge to the next depot. He is the first man to die.

March 1912: Scott is hopeful that there will be dogs at the next depot. Unfortunately, the back-up crew has left the dogs at another depot, 72 miles from Scott's location. On March 16, Oates stumbles out of the tent. He states that he is just going outside. The others know he is walking to his death. Oates is never seen again.

March 29, 1912: The blizzard rages on, and Scott makes his last journal entry. Scott, Bowers, and Wilson wait for the end in their sleeping bags. Scott is the last to die.

November 12, 1912: The search party finds Scott's tent buried in snow. The tent has collapsed over the bodies and the search party builds a snow cairn over it. A pair of crossed skis is placed on top in honor of the brave explorers.

Race to the South Pole

Compare the South Pole expeditions of Roald Amundsen and Robert Falcon Scott.
Fill in the chart with the correct information for each explorer. Use the information and
map on the other pages to help you.

	Roald Amundsen	Robert Falcon Scott
Ship's name		
Country where expedition begins, and date		
Location of base camp		
Date on which expedition from base camp to South Pole begins		
Names of men chosen to reach South Pole		
Two obstacles or tragedies on the way to the South Pole		
Date of arrival at South Pole		
Description of return journey		

Exploration by Air

The first explorer to see Antarctica from the air was Captain Robert Falcon Scott. In 1902, he went up in a tethered hot-air balloon off the Antarctic coast. Another explorer, Ernest Shackleton, also went up in the balloon and took the first aerial photos of the continent.

In the 1920s, polar explorers started using an exciting new technology—airplanes. Long-distance airplanes, which had been developed during World War I, gave explorers a perfect way to accurately map the polar regions.

Below is a timeline of some important aerial explorations from 1928 to 1948.

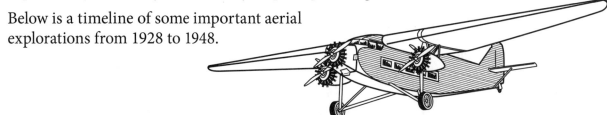

1928 • Australian George Hubert Wilkins makes the first powered flight into the Antarctic region in a monoplane, or a plane with one main set of wings.

1929 • After a 10-hour flight from a base at the Bay of Whales, American Richard E. Byrd and two others become the first to fly over the South Pole.

1935 • American Lincoln Ellsworth is the first to successfully fly across the entire continent of Antarctica. The flight is 2,300 miles (3,700 km) long.

1946 • The U.S. Navy launches a large scientific expedition called *Operation High Jump.* Over 70,000 aerial photographs are taken of the coastline for map-making purposes. Operation High Jump continues until 1947. To this day, it is the largest expedition ever launched for Antarctic exploration.

1947 • The U.S. Navy launches another expedition to Antarctica called *Operation Windmill.* The expedition continues into 1948 and consists of 500 men, two ships, three helicopters, and one airplane. This is the first time helicopters are widely used for surveying and photographing new areas of Antarctica.

Exploration by Air

A. Unscramble the words and write them on the lines to complete each sentence. Use the information on the other page to help you.

1. In 1902, Captain Robert Falcon Scott and Ernest Shackleton were the first to see

   Antarctica from a hot-air _____.

   noolalb

2. In 1928, George Hubert _____ made the first Antarctic

   flight. **lisnwik**

3. Lincoln _____ became the first to fly across Antarctica.

   telwlorsh

4. Beginning in the 1920s, _____ were used for long-range

   exploration. **apirlnase**

5. In Operation Windmill, the U.S. Navy used _____

   for exploration. **cotperlihes**

6. Richard E. Byrd and two others were the first people to fly over the

   _____.

   ostuh opel

7. The largest expedition for Antarctic exploration ever undertaken was

   Operation _____.

   hghi pumj

8. Aerial _____ were important for mapping the Antarctic

   coast. **spoothhprag**

B. Which aerial expedition do you think was the most important? Explain your answer.

_____

_____

_____

Exploration by Air

Admiral Richard E. Byrd

Richard E. Byrd was an American *admiral*, a high-ranking officer of the navy. He was also an Arctic and Antarctic explorer, aviator, and navigator. Byrd was a pioneer in modern polar exploration.

Below are highlights of Byrd's remarkable life and career.

Admiral Richard E. Byrd

- Byrd was born on October 25, 1888, in Winchester, Virginia.

- He graduated from the U.S. Naval Academy in 1912.

- He "won his wings," meaning he became a naval aviator, in 1918.

- Byrd completed his first flights, over Ellesmere Island in northern Canada and the interior of Greenland, in 1925.

- He claimed to have been the first person to fly over the North Pole in 1926. He and his pilot, Floyd Bennett, were awarded the Medal of Honor. However, many have since disputed his claim.

- Byrd established an Antarctic naval base called Little America on the Ross Ice Shelf at the Bay of Whales in 1928.

- In 1929, Byrd became the first to fly over the South Pole. His crew consisted of himself as navigator, pilot Bernt Balchen, co-pilot Harold June, and radio operator Ashley McKinley. The airplane, *Floyd Bennett,* was named after Byrd's first pilot.

- Byrd returned to Antarctica to carry out scientific research in 1933. He studied meteors, weather, and geography. Byrd operated the advanced base camp all winter by himself. He suffered from carbon monoxide poisoning, but later recovered. Byrd kept in touch with his team by using Morse Code. He wrote about his winter experience in his book *Alone*.

- Byrd commanded the U.S. Antarctic Service expedition in 1939. This expedition built another Little America, since the other had been crushed by snow and ice. Byrd sent out five major exploring parties across the continent.

- Byrd served in World War II under the Chief of Naval Operations.

- He was a leader of Operation High Jump in 1946. Over 4,700 men, 15 ships, 6 helicopters, and 23 airplanes were sent to Antarctica for exploration.

- Byrd began serving as officer in charge of the United States Antarctic Programs in 1955.

- Byrd worked on planning future Antarctic explorations until his death on March 11, 1957.

Exploration by Air

A. Number these important events in Richard E. Byrd's life in the correct chronological order. Use the information on the other page to help you.

_____ operated an Antarctic base camp by himself all winter

_____ became a naval aviator

_____ headed Operation High Jump

_____ claimed to have flown over the North Pole

_____ served in the navy in World War II

_____ graduated from the U.S. Naval Academy

_____ was the first to fly over the South Pole

B. Use the information on the other page to answer the questions.

1. Why was Byrd awarded the Medal of Honor?

   _____

2. What experience did Byrd write about in his book _Alone_?

   _____

   _____

C. What do you think was Byrd's biggest accomplishment? Explain your answer.

   _____

   _____

Review

Use words from the box to complete the crossword puzzle.

Belgica

Byrd

Heroic

Island

Scott

seal

South Pole

Unknown

Across

2. Ernest Shackleton saved his crew, who had been stranded on Elephant _____.

4. Robert Falcon _____ died on his return from an unsuccessful attempt to be the first person to reach the South Pole.

5. The period when Antarctic explorers traveled to the interior of the continent was called the _____ Age.

7. A ship named the _____ was trapped in pack ice for a year.

Down

1. *Terra Australis Incognita* is Latin for _____ Southern Land.

3. Explorer Roald Amundsen was the first to reach the _____.

6. James Weddell discovered a new type of _____ on the islands north of the Antarctic Peninsula.

7. Richard _____ was the first person to fly over the South Pole.

Antarctica Today

This section introduces students to the different activities taking place on Antarctica today, and the ways in which people are utilizing the continent for research and tourism. Students learn that Antarctica is not owned by any nation, but rather shared for peaceful purposes. Students find out about international research stations, the scientists who work there, and the telecommunication systems that keep the scientists in touch with the rest of the world. They also discover that Antarctica has become a thriving tourist destination.

Each skill in this section is based on the following National Geography Standards:

Essential Element 4: Human Systems

Standard 13: How the forces of cooperation and conflict among people influence the division and control of Earth's surface

Essential Element 6: The Uses of Geography

Standard 18: How to apply geography to interpret the present and plan for the future

CONTENTS

Overview

Antarctica has the smallest human population of any continent in the world. There are no countries on Antarctica and no permanent residents. Technically, Antarctica has a population of zero. The only people who live and work on the continent are scientists and others who help run the research stations, and they stay for only short periods of time.

Scientists drill into the Antarctic ice for samples to study.

Scientific Research Stations

Scientists and other people who work in Antarctica spend most of their time living at research stations. More than 40 year-round international research stations are located on the continent. All the nations that have research stations on Antarctica have signed a treaty to establish and maintain Antarctica as a continent for peace and science.

Women Scientists

Until the 1960s, all the U.S. research scientists in Antarctica were male. In 1969, a four-woman scientific team from Ohio State University was granted permission to do research in Antarctica. Currently, women scientists make up 30% of the important personnel at the stations.

Communication Systems

Antarctica is very remote, making communication difficult. The research stations and ships in Antarctic waters use satellites for Internet and telephone services. Radio and television stations at the research facilities also depend on satellite technology. The scientists at the stations work closely with NASA and private companies to receive the latest in satellite technology.

Tourism in Antarctica

You don't have to be a scientist to go to Antarctica today. Between 2009 and 2010, over 36,000 tourists visited Antarctica. Some cruised the Antarctic waters, some visited the Antarctic Peninsula, and some even trekked to the South Pole.

Overview

Fill in the bubble to answer each question or complete each sentence.

1. How many countries make up the continent of Antarctica?

   Ⓐ 0

   Ⓑ 12

   Ⓒ 23

   Ⓓ 40

2. The majority of the people who live in Antarctica are _____.

   Ⓐ tourists

   Ⓑ sailors

   Ⓒ women

   Ⓓ scientists

3. _____ communication systems make all other forms of communication possible in Antarctica.

   Ⓐ Radio

   Ⓑ Satellite

   Ⓒ Telephone

   Ⓓ Television

4. In _____, the first U.S. women scientists were allowed to do research in Antarctica.

   Ⓐ 1949

   Ⓑ 1960

   Ⓒ 1969

   Ⓓ 1985

5. Which statement is true about tourism in Antarctica?

   Ⓐ Tourists must help the scientists do research while visiting Antarctica.

   Ⓑ Most tourists who come to Antarctica trek to the South Pole.

   Ⓒ Tourists can sail in the Antarctic waters but may not set foot on the continent.

   Ⓓ In the 2009–2010 tourist season, more than 36,000 people visited Antarctica.

Claims to Antarctica

International Geophysical Year

Between July 1957 and December 1958, a cooperative scientific project was formed called the International Geophysical Year (IGY). The purpose of the project was for scientists around the world to study Earth and share their findings. More than 10,000 scientists from 67 countries participated in the program. About 2,500 IGY stations were set up throughout the world, with more than 50 located on Antarctica and its nearby islands. Researchers from 12 countries—Argentina, Australia, Belgium, Chile, France, Japan, New Zealand, Norway, Russia, South Africa, the United Kingdom, and the United States—studied the weather, glaciers, volcanoes, and other features of Antarctica.

Seven of the 12 countries studying Antarctica during the project claimed parts of the continent as their national territory. These countries were Argentina, Australia, Chile, France, New Zealand, Norway, and the United Kingdom. The other five countries did not recognize these claims.

Antarctic Treaty

In 1959, officials of the 12 countries that were studying Antarctica signed a treaty called the Antarctic Treaty. This treaty provided guidelines for territorial claims, as well as how Antarctic land should be used in the future. The guidelines specified the following:

- Existing claims to territories in Antarctica would not be acknowledged. Any new claims would be prohibited.
- Antarctica would be used for peaceful purposes only, such as exploration, research, and tourism.
- Scientists would share any knowledge that resulted from their studies.
- No military forces could enter Antarctica, except to assist scientific expeditions.
- Use of nuclear weapons and disposal of radioactive wastes in Antarctica was prohibited.

Peace and Science

In 1991, the Antarctic Treaty nations signed another agreement called the Madrid Protocol. This agreement defined Antarctica as a natural reserve devoted to peace and science. It prohibited taking minerals from the area and established strict rules to protect the environment.

By 2009, 47 countries had signed the Antarctic Treaty. The participating nations have helped to establish and maintain Antarctica as a continent where people from all over the world work together to gain knowledge instead of competing with each other for land and resources.

Claims to Antarctica

A. Use the information on the other page to answer the questions.

1. What was the purpose of the International Geophysical Year?

   _____

2. How many IGY countries sent researchers to Antarctica? How many scientific stations were established there?

   _____

3. Name the seven countries that had claimed parts of Antarctica by 1959.

   _____

   _____

4. What was the purpose of the Antarctic Treaty?

   _____

   _____

B. Read each statement. Circle **yes** if it is true or **no** if it is false. Use the information on the other page to help you.

1. When a new country signs the Antarctic Treaty, it is allowed to claim parts of Antarctica as its national territory.   **Yes**   **No**

2. Antarctica can be used only for peaceful purposes.   **Yes**   **No**

3. Scientists must share knowledge from their Antarctic studies.   **Yes**   **No**

4. Military forces may not enter Antarctica for any reason.   **Yes**   **No**

5. The Antarctic Treaty outlaws the use of nuclear weapons and the disposal of radioactive wastes in Antarctica.   **Yes**   **No**

6. The Madrid Protocol was created by nations that did not want to sign the Antarctic Treaty.   **Yes**   **No**

Scientific Research Stations

The scientists that come to Antarctica represent almost every scientific field, from geology and oceanography to astronomy and biology. Because of Antarctica's unique physical features and climate, scientific research can be carried out there that cannot be done anywhere else on Earth. For example, because Antarctica is dark for six months of the year, it is an ideal spot for astronomers to study objects in space. And research of the ice in Antarctica is helping scientists understand global climate change.

Approximately 30 nations operate scientific research stations in Antarctica. There are about 4,000 people who stay at the stations during the summer and about 1,000 in the winter. There are more than 40 permanent research stations that operate year-round in Antarctica and on nearby islands. The United States has three of these permanent stations.

The map below shows some of the major research stations in Antarctica.

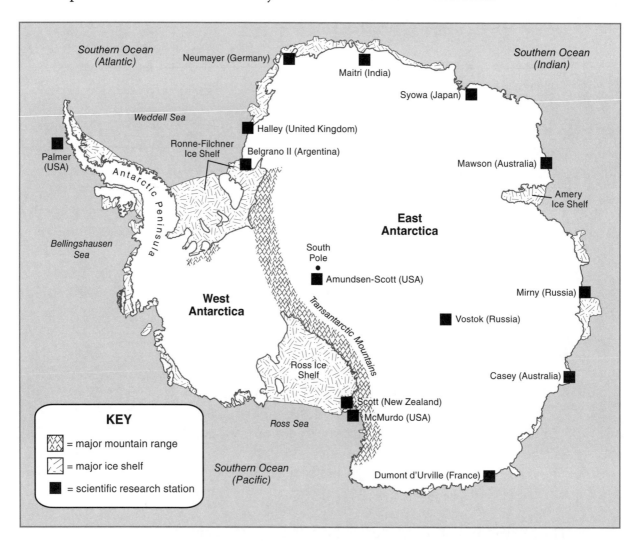

Scientific Research Stations

Answer the questions. Use the information and map on the other page to help you.

1. During which part of the year are there more people   _____
   living in Antarctica?

2. What are the names of the three U.S. research stations shown on the map?

   _____

3. Where is the Amundsen-Scott Station located?

   _____

4. What are the only two countries with research stations located in inland areas?

   _____

5. Which countries have research stations close to the Ross Ice Shelf?

   _____

6. Where is the Mawson Research Station located?

   _____

7. Besides the United States, which other countries have more than one station
   shown on the map?

   _____

8. Name two features of Antarctica that make it an ideal place to do certain kinds
   of research.

   _____

   _____

   _____

Scientific Research Stations

McMurdo Research Station

McMurdo Station is one of the three permanent U.S. stations in Antarctica. It was established in 1956 and has grown from just a few buildings to the largest station on the continent. It is named for Lieutenant Archibald McMurdo, who was on Captain James Clark Ross's ship the *Terror* in 1841.

McMurdo Station is built on the bare volcanic rock of Ross Island. The station overlooks McMurdo Sound and the Ross Ice Shelf, and is not far from Mount Erebus.

McMurdo Station is informally known as "Mac Town." There are more than 100 buildings at the site. Repair garages, dormitories, warehouses, a firehouse, and a power plant are located there. It also has a post office, barbershop, chapel, and medical facility. For fun, there are stores, radio and TV stations, and a gym. During the summer, about 1,100 people live there.

The only harbor in Antarctica is located at McMurdo Station. The station also has three airfields and a helicopter pad. Several times a week, large ships carry people and supplies to the station and leave with waste materials and scientific samples. A water distillation plant changes salty seawater into fresh water. A greenhouse supplies the station with fresh vegetables.

The McMurdo Research Station is an impressive scientific base. At the Crary Lab, many different kinds of scientists carry out experiments. There are ecologists who study the environment, geologists who study rocks and minerals, meteorologists who research climate and weather, glaciologists who study snow and ice, and astronomers who learn about the stars and planets. The Crary Lab also has its own aquarium so that marine biologists can study plants and animals of the sea.

The last flight out of McMurdo every year occurs in February, leaving only about 125 people at the station for the winter. This crew must keep the station running until McMurdo reopens for the summer. The workers withstand months of frigid temperatures that average –6°F (–21°C), high winds, and total darkness.

Scientific Research Stations

A. Write three questions about McMurdo Station that can be answered using the information on the other page. Then answer the questions.

1. _____

_____

_____

2. _____

_____

_____

3. _____

_____

_____

B. Next to each type of scientist that works at McMurdo Station, write the letter of the clue that describes that field. Use the information on the other page to help you.

_____ 1. marine biologist

_____ 2. ecologist

_____ 3. geologist

_____ 4. glaciologist

_____ 5. meteorologist

_____ 6. astronomer

a. a scientist who studies weather and climate

b. a scientist who studies ocean plants and animals

c. a scientist who studies ice and snow

d. a scientist who studies stars and planets

e. a scientist who studies rocks, minerals, and landforms

f. a scientist who studies the relationship between living things and their environment

Women Scientists in Antarctica

For many years, women were not always permitted to go to Antarctica. The continent was long considered a place for only the strongest of men. In 1956, when the U.S. Navy established McMurdo Station as a military outpost, women were not even allowed on navy ships.

The First Four-Woman Team

In 1969, the navy agreed to let a few women go to Antarctica. A group of four women from Ohio State University were the first all-female team to be chosen to go to Antarctica.

From left to right: Kay Lindsay, Terry Tickhill Terrell, Lois Jones, and Eileen McSaveney

Dr. Lois Jones, a geochemist, was selected as the leader of the team. Kay Lindsay, a biologist, and Eileen McSaveney, a glacial geologist, were also on the team. Terry Tickhill Terrell, a 19-year-old chemistry major at Ohio State, applied for the research expedition and was invited by Dr. Jones to join the group as a field assistant. The team of women left for a four-month mission to the McMurdo Dry Valleys in October 1969.

Research on McMurdo's Dry Valleys

The McMurdo Dry Valleys are the largest ice-free regions of Antarctica. The valley floors are covered with loose gravel and large rocks. Bacteria have been found living in the valleys. Scientists think these bacteria-filled valleys are the same kind of environment that might exist on Mars. Research of the bacteria in the rocks has been an important source of information for considering the possibility of life on Mars.

The four-woman team worked in the Dry Valleys, breaking rocks and hauling them away to send for chemical analysis. The women endured high winds that blew sand into all of their clothing and food. The team even survived a helicopter crash. The men at the research station were impressed with the hard work and stamina of these women scientists on Antarctica.

Forty Years of Women Researchers

In 2009, the 40th anniversary of women conducting research in Antarctica was celebrated. Jones, Lindsay, McSaveney, and Terrell were some of the first women to work on Antarctica, but definitely not the last. Today, about one-third of the scientists on Antarctica are women. Some of them head research stations and lead major expeditions.

The 7 Continents: Antarctica • EMC 3736 • © Evan-Moor Corp.

Women Scientists in Antarctica

Pretend you are writing an article for the *Antarctic Sun*, McMurdo Station's newspaper. Your assignment is to write a short piece about the first American women in Antarctica and the work they did there. Explain how the women contributed to Antarctic exploration and the impact they had on future research. Use the information on the other page to help you. Include a title, your name as the author, and a two-column article.

The Antarctic Sun

_____

_____

_____	_____
_____	_____
_____	_____
_____	_____
_____	_____
_____	_____
_____	_____
_____	_____
_____	_____
_____	_____
_____	_____

Antarctic Time

The World's Time Zones

The world is divided into 24 time zones. These zones follow the lines of longitude, beginning at the prime meridian at 0°. There are 12 time zones west of the prime meridian and 12 time zones east of the prime meridian. Each of these time zones is 15° of longitude and one hour apart.

SANAE (South Africa)
8:00 p.m.

O'Higgins (Chile)
2:00 p.m.

Halley (United
Kingdom)
6:00 p.m.

Syowa (Japan)
9:00 p.m.

Palmer
(USA)
2:00 p.m.

Belgrano II
(Argentina)
3:00 p.m.

Mawson (Australia)
12:00 p.m.

Davis (Australia)
1:00 a.m.

Amundsen-Scott (USA)
6:00 a.m.

Mirny
(Russia)
12:00 a.m.

Vostok (Russia)
12:00 a.m.

Casey
(Australia)
2:00 a.m.

McMurdo (USA)
6:00 a.m.

Dumont d'Urville
(France)
4:00 a.m.

This map shows the different time zones that various research stations in Antarctica choose to use.

South Pole Time

The South Pole is where all of the lines of longitude meet. That makes it very confusing for measuring time. At the South Pole, people could be in all 24 time zones within a few seconds! Because of this, people working in Antarctica can actually choose any time zone in the world to use for their clocks.

Choosing a Time Zone

Some research stations set their clocks according to the time zone of the country that operates the research station. For example, the United Kingdom's Halley Station sets its clocks to the time zone of London, England.

Other research stations do not use the same time zone as their home country. Instead, they choose to use the same time as the country of their nearest place of departure before reaching Antarctica. For example, two American research stations—Amundsen-Scott and McMurdo—use New Zealand Standard Time (NZST). That is because the scientists depart for Antarctica from Christchurch, New Zealand. The U.S. Palmer Station on the Antarctic Peninsula uses the country of Chile's time zone because scientists headed for the Palmer Station leave from South America. This makes it easier to coordinate shipments of supplies and equipment from the departure point.

Antarctic Time

Read each clue below. Write the correct word on the numbered lines. Then use the numbers to crack the code!

1. The world's time zones are each one _____ apart.

   ___ ___ ___ ___
   1   8   4   7

2. At the South Pole, all the lines of _____ meet.

   ___ ___ ___ ___ ___ ___ ___ ___ ___
   11 8   16 20 18 5   4   14 13

3. At the South Pole, you can be in _____ time zones within a few seconds.

   ___ ___ ___ ___ ___ ___   ___ ___ ___ ___
   5   3   13 9   5   2   12 8   4   7

4. The Russian station, _____, is six hours behind McMurdo Station.

   ___ ___ ___ ___ ___ ___
   15 8   6   5   8   19

5. The McMurdo Station uses NZST, which is New Zealand _____ Time.

   ___ ___ ___ ___ ___ ___ ___ ___
   6   5   17 9   14 17 7   14

Crack the Code!

Many stations in Antarctica do not use _____ time.

___ ___ ___ ___ ___ ___ ___ ___   ___ ___ ___ ___ ___ ___ ___
14 17 2   11 18 20 1   5   6   17 15 18 9   20 6

Name _____

Satellite Communication

A lot of data is sent back and forth between scientists on Antarctica and the people they work with in their home countries. In order to transmit information quickly, the researchers depend on modern *telecommunication* systems. *Telecommunication* means communicating over long distances, especially by electronic means. Scientists on Antarctica use cellular telephone and Internet service provided by *satellites*, which are large pieces of equipment that orbit Earth. U.S. research stations on Antarctica rely on satellites from NASA (National Aeronautics and Space Administration), the USAF (U.S. Air Force), and NOAA (National Oceanic and Atmospheric Administration) to communicate. Radio and television stations, and even the *Antarctic Sun* newspaper at McMurdo Station, depend on satellites to transmit their data and news electronically.

How Communication Satellites Work

Communication satellites bounce signals from one side of Earth to the other. First, a ground-based transmitter dish from Antarctica beams a signal to the satellite. This transmission is called an uplink. The satellite then boosts the signal and sends it back down to Earth to a receiving dish in the United States. This is called a downlink. The whole process happens using radio waves, which travel at the speed of light.

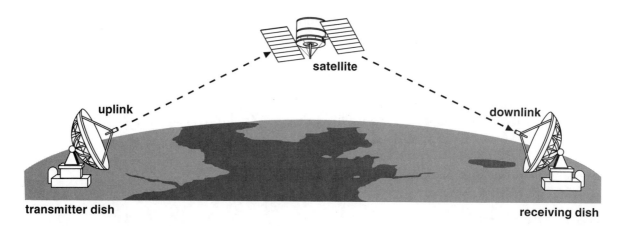

satellite

uplink   downlink

transmitter dish   receiving dish

Keeping Communication Current

Communication satellites give scientists the ability to return scientific data to the U.S. for about five hours each day. One of the most important satellites for researchers from the United States was TDRS 1 (NASA's Tracking and Data Relay Satellite). It began orbiting in space in 1983 and was used in Antarctic research from 1998 to 2009. In June 2010, TDRS 1 was shut down. The satellite TDRS 3 is being used as a backup until a replacement satellite is launched.

The United States' Antarctic research depends on being able to communicate with the world at large. NASA and private companies are designing new satellites to replace the aging ones.

Satellite Communication

A. Next to each term, write the letter of the clue that describes it. Use the information on the other page to help you.

_____ 1. TDRS 1

_____ 2. telecommunication

_____ 3. *Antarctic Sun*

_____ 4. NASA

_____ 5. transmitter dish

_____ 6. receiving dish

_____ 7. USAF

_____ 8. radio waves

_____ 9. NOAA

_____ 10. satellite

a. something that sends a radio signal

b. waves of energy that travel at the speed of light

c. the government agency that oversees space travel and research

d. McMurdo Station's newspaper

e. a piece of equipment that orbits Earth

f. electronic communication at a distance

g. the government agency that researches weather and the oceans

h. an important satellite once used by U.S. Antarctic research stations

i. something that picks up a radio signal

j. the United States Air Force

B. Name three ways communication satellites help scientists and other workers at the Antarctic research stations.

1. _____

2. _____

3. _____

Tourism in Antarctica

Although Antarctic tourism began in the late 1950s, there were very few visitors to the cold continent until the early 1990s, when tourism began to increase rapidly. From 1990 to 1991, 4,698 tourists visited Antarctica. In the 2009–2010 season, the number was up to 36,875. Each year, there are far more tourists than scientists and support staff in Antarctica.

Travelers go to Antarctica for adventure and to experience one of the world's most remote and unspoiled places. They come to see colossal icebergs and fascinating wildlife such as penguins, seals, and whales.

Most ships carrying tourists leave from Tierra del Fuego in South America and sail to the area around the Antarctic Peninsula. A few ships leave from Australia or New Zealand and visit the Ross Sea region. Trips are taken from November to March, during the Antarctic summer when the coastal areas are free of ice.

In the past, tourists traveled only in small or medium-sized ships that carried fewer than 200 passengers. However, in recent years, larger cruise ships carrying anywhere from 500 to 3,000 passengers have begun traveling to Antarctica. The growing number of tourists and larger ships in Antarctica present both environmental and safety challenges.

Many people worry about increased pollution from ship fuel and the waste that is discharged into the ocean around the continent. An oil spill from a large ship would be disastrous to Antarctica. Also, many tourists want to visit the most scenic and wildlife-rich areas. But with more people going ashore, there's a higher chance of disturbing the landscape and the animals.

Concerns have also been raised about the lack of safety precautions for tourists, such as lifeboats and clear emergency procedures. Many of the enormous ships now sailing in Antarctic waters were not built to withstand being hit by ice. If ships do run into trouble, as did the *MS Explorer,* which sunk in 2007, rescue efforts are very costly and difficult.

In 2006, the nations of the Antarctic Treaty warned that Antarctic tourism needed to be limited. They suggested tougher inspections of ships, a ban on ships not strong enough for ice, and forcing ships to travel in pairs in case one gets into trouble. Only time will tell if Antarctica will be able to remain a place devoted to peace and science, or whether tourists will threaten the preservation of the continent.

Tourism in Antarctica

A. Read each statement. Circle **yes** if it is true or **no** if it is false. Use the information on the other page to help you.

1. Most tourists take off from Tierra del Fuego to visit Antarctica.   **Yes**   **No**

2. Large ships can carry up to 3,000 passengers to Antarctica.   **Yes**   **No**

3. More than 36,000 tourists visited Antarctica between 1990 and 1991.   **Yes**   **No**

4. Antarctic tourism began in the late 1950s.   **Yes**   **No**

5. Tourists typically visit Antarctica during the months of April to October.   **Yes**   **No**

6. Antarctic tourists visit the continent mostly to conduct scientific experiments.   **Yes**   **No**

7. More tourists come to Antarctica than scientists do.   **Yes**   **No**

8. The *MS Explorer* sunk in Antarctic waters in 2007.   **Yes**   **No**

9. Most tourist ships that go to Antarctica are built to withstand a collision with ice.   **Yes**   **No**

10. Member nations of the Antarctic Treaty are concerned about the effects of tourism on Antarctica.   **Yes**   **No**

B. Name two ways that increased tourism could harm the Antarctic environment.

_____

_____

_____

Review

Use words from the box to complete the crossword puzzle.

Antarctic

McMurdo

research

satellites

summer

time

tourists

women

Across

1. Many thousands of _____ visit Antarctica every year.

4. People in Antarctica can choose which _____ zone to set their clocks to.

5. Most scientists live at _____ stations while conducting their experiments on Antarctica.

7. Jones, Lindsay, McSaveney, and Terrell were some of the first _____ to go to Antarctica.

8. In 1959, 12 countries signed the _____ Treaty.

Down

2. Most people come to Antarctica in the _____, when the temperatures are more mild.

3. _____ Station is the largest research station in Antarctica.

6. Scientists use _____ to communicate their findings to the outside world.

Antarctica's Wildlife

This section introduces students to the small and large animals that are uniquely adapted to Antarctica's frigid waters and coastal areas. Students learn about the importance of the Antarctic food web and find out that most Antarctic animals are dependent on small shrimp-like creatures called krill. Students identify the different birds, fish, seals, and whales that inhabit Antarctica. They also discover the strange sea animals that live in the depths of the vast Southern Ocean.

Each skill in this section is based on the following National Geography Standards:

Essential Element 3: Physical Systems

Standard 8: The characteristics and spatial distribution of ecosystems on Earth's surface

Essential Element 5: Environment and Society

Standard 16: The changes that occur in the meaning, use, distribution, and importance of resources

CONTENTS

Overview

Despite Antarctica's harsh environment, its coastal areas and surrounding waters are home to some of the most fascinating wildlife on Earth. From tiny shrimp-like creatures called *krill* to giants such as the blue whale, Antarctica's frigid seas and icy lands contain more life than you might expect.

Penguins and Seabirds

Penguins are one of the most familiar animal species on Antarctica. They are flightless birds that spend most of their lives on pack ice and in the coastal waters of the Southern Ocean. Six kinds of penguins live in Antarctica—the Adélie, chinstrap, emperor, gentoo, king, and macaroni penguins.

Many flying seabirds also live in Antarctica. The largest of these is the wandering albatross. This bird commonly follows ships, looking for food. It also dives into the water to catch squid.

Seals

Antarctica has six species of seals. They are the Antarctic fur, crabeater, leopard, Ross, southern elephant, and Weddell seals. These mammals spend most of their time in the water, although they do rest on land or on pack ice. The gigantic southern elephant seal prefers lying on the beach. Most seals feed on fish and squid. However, the leopard seal also eats other types of seals and penguins.

Giants of the Sea

There are two types of whales that swim in the Southern Ocean. *Baleen whales* are whales that do not have teeth. They filter food from the water using baleen, stiff fingernail-like material that hangs in layers from their upper jaw. There are six types of baleen whales in the Antarctic, including the blue whale and humpback whale.

Whales that have teeth hunt larger prey. There are five kinds of *toothed whales* in the Southern Ocean, including the sperm whale and orca. The large sperm whale dives to feed on its favorite foods—large fish and squid. Groups of orcas, also known as killer whales, hunt large prey such as the blue whale calf.

Strange Creatures

Some unusual animals are in the deep waters of the Southern Ocean. One type of fish hibernates, and another type is colorless. There are giant squid and venomous octopuses. There are also some strange smaller creatures, such as the sea spider and sea pig.

Overview

Fill in the bubble to answer each question or complete each sentence.

1. Which animal does *not* live in the deep waters of the Southern Ocean?

   Ⓐ sea spider

   Ⓑ venomous octopus

   Ⓒ southern elephant seal

   Ⓓ sea pig

2. Which of these animals can fly?

   Ⓐ emperor penguin

   Ⓑ chinstrap penguin

   Ⓒ wandering albatross

   Ⓓ krill

3. The _____ seal feeds on other types of seals.

   Ⓐ Antarctic fur

   Ⓑ leopard

   Ⓒ southern elephant

   Ⓓ crabeater

4. Which statement is true about penguins?

   Ⓐ There are six kinds of penguins in Antarctica.

   Ⓑ There are five kinds of penguins in Antarctica.

   Ⓒ Penguins always stay on ice and avoid the water.

   Ⓓ Penguins swoop down from the air to catch fish.

5. Which type of whale filters its food from the water?

   Ⓐ toothed whale

   Ⓑ sperm whale

   Ⓒ killer whale

   Ⓓ baleen whale

Antarctica's Food Web

All the plants and animals that live in a particular place depend on one another as sources of food. These plants and animals can be organized into a *food chain*, or a group of living things shown in the order in which each member feeds on another one. An animal that is not eaten by any other animals is said to be "at the top of the food chain." For example, in Antarctica, orcas eat seals, and seals eat fish. However, no animals eat orcas, so orcas are at the top of the food chain.

Most environments have more than one food chain. For instance, in Antarctica, orcas eat penguins, and penguins eat fish. But orcas can also eat leopard seals, which can also eat fish. These overlapping and connected food chains form a giant *food web*. In a food web, more than one animal can be considered "at the top" as long as no other animals eat them.

The diagram below is an example of an Antarctic food web. The arrows point from the living things that are being eaten to the living things that do the eating.

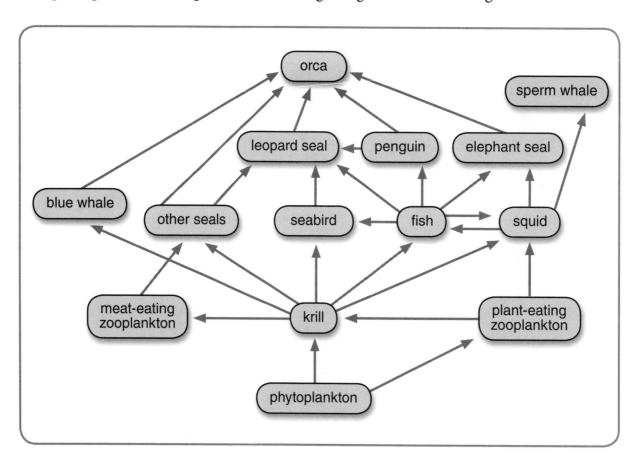

At the base of the Antarctic food web are *phytoplankton*. These are microscopic, single-celled plants that drift near the ocean's surface. All life in Antarctica depends on these minute creatures.

Antarctica's Food Web

A. Use the food web on the other page to help you answer the questions below.

1. Which animal is eaten by the most other animals
   on this food web?   _____

2. Which animal eats seabirds?   _____

3. What is the largest animal that eats krill?   _____

4. Which two animals eat penguins?

   _____

5. Which two creatures are eaten by krill?

   _____

6. Which two animals are at the top of the Antarctic food web?

   _____

7. Fish are eaten by how many animals? Name them.

   _____

8. According to the web, which three animals are eaten by squid?

   _____

B. Explain the difference between a food chain and a food web.

_____

_____

_____

_____

Antarctic Krill

Krill are tiny shrimp-like creatures. Though small, they are of huge importance in the Antarctic food web. Without krill, most of the animals in the Southern Ocean would not survive.

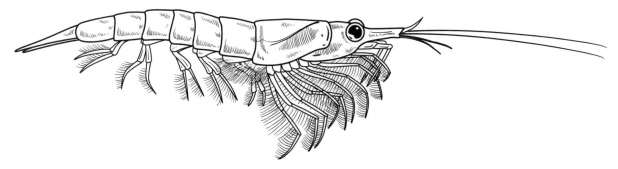

Fast Facts About Krill

- A krill is a small *crustacean*. A crustacean is an animal that has a hard shell, legs with joints, and a body that is divided into segments. Other crustaceans include crabs, shrimp, and lobsters.

- Antarctic krill are among the largest of the 85 known krill species. Each krill is 2 inches (5 cm) long and weighs only 0.035 ounces (1 g).

- Krill are *translucent*, which means that some light shows through their skin. The shells of krill are pink with red spots.

- During the day, krill stay about 320 feet (100 m) below the surface of the ocean, where the darkness protects them from predators.

- At night, krill come out to feed on phytoplankton, the microscopic, single-celled plants that drift near the ocean's surface.

- Krill can go without eating for up to 200 days.

- Many predators feed on krill. These predators include fish, birds, penguins, seals, and baleen whales. A blue whale can eat 8,000 pounds (3,600 kg) of krill in one day.

- The average life span of a krill is 5 to 7 years.

- The female krill produces up to 10,000 eggs each summer. The eggs are laid at the surface of the water but then sink to great depths. The hatchlings swim back up to the surface to feed.

- Krill swim in groups called *swarms*. Some swarms of krill can spread across more than 174 square miles (450 square km).

- Estimates of the amount of Antarctic krill in the Southern Ocean range from 125 million tons (113 million metric tons) to 6 billion tons (5.4 billion metric tons).

Name _____

Antarctic Krill

A. Unscramble the words and write them on the blanks to complete the sentences. Use the information on the other page to help you.

1. Krill belong to the _____ family.
   nacecaruts

2. Krill feed on tiny plants called _____.
   thanpypoltonk

3. The blue whale is a major _____ of Antarctic krill.
   aporterd

4. The bodies of Antarctic krill are _____, with a pink shell.
   lurtecnants

5. A female krill produces up to ten _____ eggs every year.
   osudatnh

6. Krill swim in large groups called _____.
   sarmsw

B. The Antarctic krill is about the size of a large paper clip. Trace around a large paper clip. Draw a krill beside it to show its relative size. Write a caption under the illustration that describes the length of an Antarctic krill.

Paper Clip	Antarctic Krill

_____

_____

The Wandering Albatross

The Southern Ocean is home to many kinds of seabirds. The largest and most majestic of these birds is the wandering albatross. The wandering albatross is the most famous albatross of the Antarctic.

Physical Characteristics

The wandering albatross is 42 to 53 inches (107 to 135 cm) in length and weighs between 18 and 20 pounds (8 and 9 kg). Its body is snowy white with black feathers at the tip of the tail. Its wings are black and white on top and white underneath, with a narrow black rim at the tips. The wandering albatross has the largest wingspan of any bird in the world—11 feet (3 m) from tip to tip!

Master Glider

The albatross spends over 80% of its life at sea, visiting land only for breeding. It can fly at speeds of up to 87 mph (140 km/h) over long distances. An albatross may travel 5,000 miles (8,000 km) in a week in search of food. The albatross can live up to 60 years, and, in that lifetime, will have traveled millions of miles.

A Rich Diet

The wandering albatross prefers to eat squid and fish. The albatross snaps up its food when the fish or squid comes up to the surface of the ocean. The bird can also dive into the water to capture its prey. However, the wandering albatross will also eat *carrion*, or dead animals left by others. It is known for following fishing boats to feast on the remains of the catch that has been dumped into the ocean.

Loyal Parents

A male and female albatross mate for life. The pair builds a nest on a high, windy spot on an island. The female lays one egg every other year, and parents take turns sitting on the egg for an average of 78 days. When the chick hatches, it is fluffy and white. The mother and father albatross fly great distances to find food for their chick. The chick is fed partly digested squid or fish mixed with oils from the parent's stomach. The chick stays in or near the nest for about nine months. Then, when the chick becomes a *fledgling,* or a young bird that has learned to fly, it leaves its parents and heads out to the Southern Ocean to live on its own.

The Wandering Albatross

A. Use the information on the other page to help you answer the questions below.

1. What is the wingspan of the wandering albatross?   _____

2. What two foods does the albatross prefer to eat?   _____

3. How many miles might an albatross travel in one week? _____

4. Where does the albatross spend 80% of its time?   _____

5. What is a chick that is ready to fly called?   _____

6. Name two ways that albatross parents care for their eggs and chicks.

   _____

   _____

B. Use the information in the paragraph below to answer the questions.

Early sailors believed that seeing an albatross would bring them good luck. They also believed that if someone killed the bird, it would bring danger to the ship. In the poem *The Rime of the Ancient Mariner*, an albatross starts to follow a ship. A sailor shoots the albatross with an arrow, which curses the ship. To punish the man, his fellow sailors make him wear the dead albatross around his neck. To this day, the saying "an albatross around one's neck" means that a person carries a heavy burden, or a reminder of something he or she did wrong.

1. Why did the sailors in the poem punish the crew member who killed the albatross?

   _____

   _____

2. Can you think of another poem or story where a character had an albatross around his or her neck, or carried a heavy burden or a reminder of a bad deed? Name the story and what the character did wrong.

   _____

   _____

Penguins of Antarctica

Penguins are probably the most well-known animal of Antarctica. They are flightless birds that spend most of their lives in the ocean. Even though they cannot fly, they dart through the water, diving for food. On land, they stand upright and waddle on their webbed feet.

Six kinds of penguins breed on the continent of Antarctica and its surrounding islands. They are the Adélie, chinstrap, emperor, gentoo, king, and macaroni penguins. Rockhopper penguins are sometimes included on the list of Antarctic penguins because they inhabit the waters between South America and Antarctica.

All penguins have the following characteristics in common:

- Penguins can swim for many hours at about 8 mph (13 km/h). They can reach three times that speed in short bursts. In order to breathe, penguins leap into the air from under the water about once a minute.

- Penguins are covered with short, thick feathers that form a waterproof coat. They have an extra layer of long, downy feathers below their waterproof feathers. Under those feathers is a layer of fat called *blubber*. The feathers and blubber keep the penguins warm.

- At the base of their tails, penguins have an oil gland. They dip their beaks into the gland and then spread the oil over their feathers. The oil keeps the feathers waterproof.

- Penguins eat krill, fish, and squid. They use their spiny tongues to grasp their prey and chomp down using powerful jaws.

- Penguins have excellent underwater vision. Their eyes are sensitive to violet, green, and blue light. Krill give off a blue-green light, so they are easy prey for penguins. On land, penguins are nearsighted, meaning that they cannot see objects at a distance very clearly.

- Like other seabirds, penguins have a salt gland, which extracts excess salt from their blood when they swallow sea water.

- Penguins are sociable animals and are also good parents. They breed in large colonies called *rookeries*. They never leave eggs or young chicks unattended.

- Penguins lost the ability to fly millions of years ago. As they spent more time in the water, their wings began to look more like flippers. These limbs helped penguins "fly" underwater using the same motion that other birds use to fly in the air.

Penguins of Antarctica

Look at the pictures to identify the physical differences between the six kinds of Antarctic penguins. Then answer the questions below. Use the information on the other page to help you.

1. What are two physical features that all six of the penguins have in common?

   _____

   _____

2. Pick two penguins. Name two features they have that are different from each other.

   _____

   _____

Penguins of Antarctica

Two of the best-known penguins on Antarctica are the Adélie penguin and the emperor penguin. The Adélie penguin is the smallest penguin on the cold continent, while the emperor is the largest.

Adélie Penguin

Habitat
- spends the winter at sea on pack ice
- nests on rocky shores around the continent in the spring

Characteristics
- adult is 30 inches (75 cm) tall and weighs 11 lbs (5 kg)
- black and white feathers
- white ring around eyes; reddish beak with black tip

Diet
- krill, fish, and squid

Reproduction
- builds nest with small stones
- female lays two greenish-white eggs; parents take turns sitting on the eggs
- eggs hatch after 35 days
- chicks huddle in nursery groups called *creches* for warmth and safety

Behavior
- nests in very large colonies
- swims up to 185 miles (300 km) round-trip to obtain a meal for growing chicks
- steals stones from other penguins' nests

Enemies
- leopard seals and killer whales
- seabirds that steal eggs and young chicks

Emperor Penguin

Habitat
- Weddell and Ross seas
- forms small colonies on pack ice along the coast of Antarctica

Characteristics
- adult is 42 inches (115 cm) tall and weighs 84 lbs (38 kg)
- blackish-blue body with white chest and belly
- patches of white and yellow around ears and neck

Diet
- fish, squid, shrimp, crab, and lobster

Reproduction
- breeds in winter and has no nest
- female lays one egg and passes it to male, who balances it on his feet
- egg stays in male's brood pouch (made of thick skin and feathers) until chick hatches

Behavior
- dives deeper than any bird; often reaches 700 feet (213 m) underwater
- colonies march in long single-file line for 70 miles (113 km) to reach breeding area

Enemies
- leopard seals and killer whales
- seabirds that steal eggs and young chicks

Penguins of Antarctica

A. Use the information on the other page to help you fill out the Venn diagram comparing Adélie and emperor penguins. The middle section has been started for you.

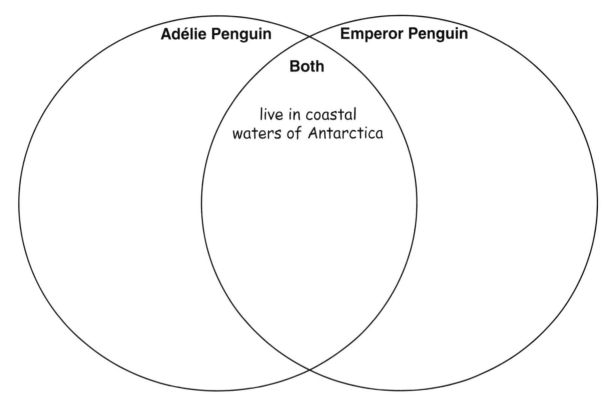

Adélie Penguin   **Emperor Penguin**

Both

live in coastal
waters of Antarctica

B. Which penguin—Adélie or emperor—is your favorite? Draw a picture of it and write a caption beside the picture. Use the information on the other page to help you.

Antarctic Seals

Antarctica has six species of seals—the leopard, Ross, crabeater, Antarctic fur, southern elephant, and Weddell seals. Each of these is uniquely adapted to the frigid waters of Antarctica, with thick layers of blubber or dense fur to keep them warm, and flippers for swimming.

Leopard Seal

Habitat
- Antarctic waters, pack-ice floes, and islands

Characteristics
- female is larger than male; she is 12 feet (3 m) long and weighs up to 1,000 lbs (454 kg)
- dark gray upper body, light gray underneath
- white throat with black spots
- large head on sleek, slender body

Diet
- krill, fish, squid, and penguins
- the only seal that eats other seals

Reproduction
- pairs come ashore only to breed
- female digs small den for single pup; pup weighs 65 lbs (29 kg) at birth
- may live up to 26 years or more

Behavior
- solitary and aggressive
- will attack people when provoked

Enemies
- killer whales

Ross Seal

Habitat
- pack ice of Antarctic waters; is rarely seen

Characteristics
- female is larger than male; she is 7 feet (2 m) long and weighs 410 lbs (190 kg)
- short dark gray or brown fur
- brown stripes from chin to chest
- wide head, short snout, and large eyes

Diet
- mostly squid; also eats fish and krill
- can feed in deep waters, using large eyes to see underwater

Reproduction
- pups are born on pack ice and weigh 60 lbs (27 kg) at birth
- pups are weaned after 25 days

Behavior
- when disturbed, raises head and leans back with open jaws
- uses siren-like call to attract mate or warn off others

Enemies
- killer whales and leopard seals

Antarctic Seals

Crabeater Seal

Habitat
- coastal waters and pack ice surrounding the continent

Characteristics
- adult is about 10 feet (3 m) long and weighs up to 500 lbs (227 kg)
- mostly gray, but coat turns almost white in summer
- dog-like face with two rows of interlocking pointed teeth

Diet
- mostly krill; also eats fish and squid
- does not eat crab, despite its name
- uses teeth to strain krill from water
- can consume 20 to 25 times its own body weight in a year

Reproduction
- male patrols territory around mate and pup, fending off intruders
- pups are weaned at two to three weeks

Behavior
- lies on ice floes either alone or in small groups of three or four
- younger seals swim in large groups of several hundred

Enemies
- killer whales and leopard seals

Antarctic Fur Seal

Habitat
- sub-Antarctic islands of South Georgia, South Shetland, South Orkney, and South Sandwich

Characteristics
- adult male is 7 feet (2 m) long and four times heavier than female; he weighs up to 440 lbs (200 kg)
- short fur coat
- male is silvery-gray and female is grayish-brown with creamy throat and upper chest

Diet
- mostly krill; also eats fish and squid
- dives up to 300 feet (91 m) to catch prey

Reproduction
- dominant male, called a *bull*, has up to six females in group
- pups are weaned after four months

Behavior
- migrates north to warmer waters in winter
- male establishes territory by patrolling an area and fighting other bulls

Enemies
- killer whales and leopard seals

Antarctic Seals

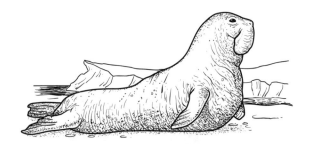

Southern Elephant Seal

Habitat
• Antarctic waters
• beaches of sub-Antarctic islands

Characteristics
• adult male is five to six times larger than female; he is 20 feet (6 m) long and weighs up to 4 tons (3.6 metric tons)
• silvery-brown skin with large, square-shaped head
• male has trunk-like snout that inflates

Diet
• large fish and squid
• occasionally penguins
• dives up to several thousand feet for as long as two hours to catch prey

Reproduction
• dominant bull looks after 50 females, or *cows*, on the beach
• pups gain 20 lbs (9 kg) each day for the first four weeks of life

Behavior
• male fights aggressively with other bulls
• when fighting, bull bends body into a U shape, balancing on chest in show of strength

Enemies
• killer whales

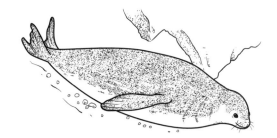

Weddell Seal

Habitat
• lives farther south than any other mammal on Earth
• spends most of its time under thick ice; comes up through cracks and blowholes to breathe and rest

Characteristics
• adults are up to 11 feet (3 m) long and weigh about 990 lbs (450 kg)
• short, dense, rust-brown fur
• small head with V-shaped nostrils

Diet
• krill, fish, and squid
• dives over 2,000 feet (610 m) and stays underwater for over an hour to catch prey

Reproduction
• mothers gather in female-only colonies to give birth
• pups weigh 60 lbs (27 kg) at birth

Behavior
• uses strong teeth to chew and scrape breathing holes in ice
• makes a variety of calls when underwater

Enemies
• no enemies, since killer whales and leopard seals do not live under thick ice

Antarctic Seals

A. Circle the name of the seal that is described by each statement. Use the information on the other pages to help you.

1. This spotted and aggressive seal eats other seals.   **elephant seal**   **leopard seal**

2. Penguins are part of the diet of this seal.   **Weddell seal**   **fur seal**

3. A siren-like call is made by this seal.   **Ross seal**   **crabeater seal**

4. This seal has a trunk-like snout.   **crabeater seal**   **elephant seal**

5. This seal has been known to attack people.   **leopard seal**   **Ross seal**

6. Rows of interlocking teeth help this seal strain krill from water.   **crabeater seal**   **leopard seal**

7. This seal migrates to warmer waters in the winter.   **elephant seal**   **fur seal**

8. This seal has a small head with V-shaped nostrils.   **Weddell seal**   **crabeater seal**

9. This seal lives where killer whales and leopard seals cannot get it.   **Ross seal**   **Weddell seal**

10. This gigantic bull prefers lying on the beach, watching over the females.   **elephant seal**   **Weddell seal**

B. Which of the six seals is the most interesting to you? Write three reasons why.

_____

_____

_____

Whales of the Southern Ocean

Eleven species of whales inhabit the Southern Ocean. Six of them are baleen whales, meaning they have no teeth. Instead, they have layers of fingernail-like material in their mouths, which they use to strain out krill from the water. The six baleen whale species in Antarctica are the blue, fin, humpback, minke, sei, and southern right whales.

Five Antarctic whales are toothed whales. They have sharp teeth and feed mostly on fish and squid. The five toothed species are the Arnoux's beaked, orca, southern bottlenose, sperm, and strap-toothed whales.

Below is a chart that describes two of the baleen and two of the toothed whale species in the Southern Ocean.

Whale	Fast Facts
Blue Whale (baleen)	• largest animal that has ever lived on Earth • adult is 85 to 100 feet (26 to 30 m) long and weighs 85 to 150 tons (77 to 136 metric tons) • baby whale, called a *calf*, is 25 feet (7 m) long and weighs 3 tons (2.7 metric tons) • feeds on 4 tons (3.6 metric tons) of krill a day
Humpback Whale (baleen)	• male is known for his long, "singing" call • adult is 40 to 50 feet (12 to 15 m) long and weighs 25 to 40 tons (23 to 36 metric tons) • calf is 12 feet (4 m) long and weighs 1 ton (0.9 metric tons) • feeds on 1.5 tons (1 metric ton) of krill a day
Sperm Whale (toothed)	• is able to dive to depths of 3,300 feet (1,000 m) • adult is 35 to 60 feet (11 to 18 m) long and weighs 35 to 45 tons (32 to 41 metric tons) • calf is 14 feet (4 m) long and weighs 1 ton (0.9 metric tons) • feeds on 1 ton (0.9 metric tons) of squid and fish a day
Orca, or Killer Whale (toothed)	• hunts in groups for large prey such as blue whale calves • adult is 23 to 32 feet (8 to 10 m) long and weighs 4 to 9 tons (3.6 to 8 metric tons) • calf is 7 feet (2 m) long and weighs 400 lbs (181 kg) • eats fish, penguins, squid, and other whales

Whales of the Southern Ocean

A. Find and circle the types of whales and their food sources in the word puzzle. Words may appear across, down, or diagonally.

```
A  N  B  F  I  S  D  E  E  J  R  C  B  A  B
B  E  W  H  S  H  R  H  M  G  W  H  C  T  O
M  S  Q  U  I  D  E  U  L  O  C  R  J  L  T
C  R  A  L  E  M  T  M  A  P  O  A  S  Y  T
D  E  I  Z  L  V  A  P  M  E  O  B  E  X  L
A  C  W  O  A  H  B  B  A  L  E  E  N  H  E
U  A  B  S  H  L  E  A  T  I  H  H  W  B  N
O  L  I  N  A  M  Z  C  J  T  P  S  E  T  O
P  F  G  P  L  F  I  K  R  I  L  L  E  G  S
A  I  X  L  E  K  U  K  L  N  O  I  D  Z  E
X  S  F  U  T  N  T  O  O  T  H  E  D  H  O
P  D  L  U  W  A  G  F  I  S  E  K  R  V  C
R  B  N  W  M  X  C  U  K  P  O  N  V  H  E
Y  A  T  E  V  J  U  P  I  I  T  E  S  S  A
M  V  E  H  Z  E  G  U  L  N  U  M  X  A  D
```

baleen

blue

bottlenose

calf

humpback

krill

orca

penguin

squid

toothed

B. Write three facts about the whales of the Southern Ocean. Use the information on the other page to help you.

1. _____

_____

2. _____

_____

3. _____

_____

Three Antarctic Fish

There are 200 species of fish found in the Southern Ocean surrounding Antarctica. Most of these species are found nowhere else in the world. Below are three kinds of fish that have *adapted,* or changed, in order to be able to live in the harsh environment of the icy Southern Ocean.

Antarctic Cod

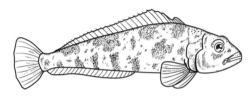

The Antarctic cod, also known as the toothfish, is the largest fish in Antarctica. It is found in the deep waters of the Southern Ocean. The fish is about 5 feet (1.5 m) long and weighs over 55 pounds (25 kg). Some Antarctic cod reach as much as 330 pounds (150 kg). Most are gray in color. However, some are speckled with black, yellow, and blue and have bright yellow fins. The Antarctic cod feeds on other fish, but it will also eat the remains of dead penguins.

Scientists have discovered that the Antarctic cod can conserve energy by entering a *dormant* state, which is similar to hibernation, in the winter. The fish has special proteins in its body that keep it from freezing in the cold water.

Blackfin Icefish

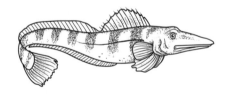

The blackfin icefish lives in the deep waters off the Antarctic Peninsula. The icefish is about 20 to 28 inches (50 to 70 cm) long and can weigh up to 8 pounds (4 kg). This fish is typically light blue with cream-colored gills. It feeds on other fish and krill.

The icefish does not have red blood cells, which means that its blood is colorless. Icefish, like the Antarctic cod, have special proteins in their blood that keep them from freezing.

Crocodile Dragonfish

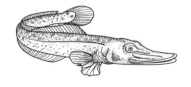

The crocodile dragonfish is a small, multicolored fish. It is only about 8 inches (20 cm) long. This funny-looking fish has a long, pointed snout but does not have a first dorsal fin, or main top fin.

The dragonfish lives in deep Antarctic waters. Because it swims near the bottom of the ocean, it does not have a swim bladder, which is the gas-filled organ that helps many fish float near the surface of the water.

Three Antarctic Fish

Read each clue below. Write the correct word on the numbered lines. Then use the numbers to crack the code!

1. Antarctic fish have ____, or changed, in order to live in the icy waters of Antarctica.

   $\overline{16}$ $\overline{13}$ $\overline{16}$ $\overline{4}$ $\overline{1}$ $\overline{12}$ $\overline{13}$

2. Antarctic cod enter a ____ state in winter so that they won't use up too much energy.

   $\overline{13}$ $\overline{5}$ $\overline{3}$ $\overline{7}$ $\overline{16}$ $\overline{6}$ $\overline{1}$

3. The ____ dragonfish has a long head with a pointed snout.

   $\overline{14}$ $\overline{3}$ $\overline{5}$ $\overline{14}$ $\overline{5}$ $\overline{13}$ $\overline{9}$ $\overline{8}$ $\overline{12}$

4. The blood of an ____ is colorless, not red.

   $\overline{9}$ $\overline{14}$ $\overline{12}$ $\overline{11}$ $\overline{9}$ $\overline{2}$ $\overline{10}$

5. Antarctic fish have special ____ in their bodies to keep them from freezing.

   $\overline{4}$ $\overline{3}$ $\overline{5}$ $\overline{1}$ $\overline{12}$ $\overline{9}$ $\overline{6}$ $\overline{2}$

6. The dragonfish has no need for a swim ____, as it lives near the sea floor.

   $\overline{15}$ $\overline{8}$ $\overline{16}$ $\overline{13}$ $\overline{13}$ $\overline{12}$ $\overline{3}$

Crack the Code!

The three kinds of fish mentioned on the other page are *piscivorous* (peh-SIV-eh-ruhs), which means they are ____.

$\overline{11}$ $\overline{9}$ $\overline{2}$ $\overline{10}$ $\overline{12}$ $\overline{16}$ $\overline{1}$ $\overline{12}$ $\overline{3}$ $\overline{2}$

The Colossal Squid

The colossal squid is also called the Antarctic squid or the giant cranch squid. Only a few specimens have ever been studied, so many things about this creature remain a mystery.

In 2007, a colossal squid became entangled in fishing lines. The squid had been eating a Patagonian toothfish. This was the largest whole specimen of a colossal squid ever caught. It was frozen and sent to New Zealand for study. The squid weighed 990 pounds (449 kg). Original estimates of its length were between 26 and 32 feet (8 to 10 m). However, after the squid died, its tentacles shrunk and its length was measured at 14 feet (4 m). Based on its size and deep pink color, scientists believe the squid lived about 3,000 to 6,000 feet (914 to 1,830 m) beneath the surface of the sea. Its eyes were as wide as dinner plates, and there were sharp hooks on the ends of its tentacles.

The diagram below shows the different parts of a colossal squid.

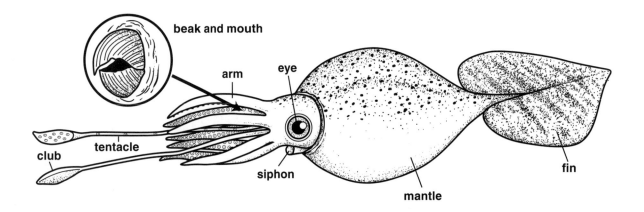

- **Tentacles:** two long, flexible limbs used for moving, feeling, and grasping

- **Clubs:** located at the end of each tentacle; have two rows of sharp, swiveling hooks

- **Arms:** eight short limbs, each with two rows of suction cups on the lower side to hold food while the squid eats

- **Beak and mouth:** parrot-like beak used for biting food

- **Eyes:** each 10 inches (25 cm) wide, the largest eyes of any creature on Earth

- **Siphon:** a tube-like organ that expels water forcefully; used for breathing, getting rid of waste, and helping to propel the squid through the sea

- **Mantle:** flexible body containing the stomach, three hearts, and other organs

- **Fins:** two flaps that help stabilize the squid while swimming

The Colossal Squid

A. Read each statement. Circle **yes** if it is true or **no** if it is false. Use the information and diagram on the other page to help you.

1. The colossal squid is also known as the Antarctic squid.   Yes   No

2. Many colossal squid have been caught in the Southern Ocean.   Yes   No

3. In 2007, a colossal squid weighing 990 pounds was caught in fishing lines.   Yes   No

4. The colossal squid has two short arms and eight long tentacles.   Yes   No

5. In the mantle of the squid, there are three stomachs and one heart.   Yes   No

6. Each eye of a colossal squid is 25 centimeters wide.   Yes   No

7. Each arm of the squid has two rows of suction cups.   Yes   No

8. At the ends of the squid's tentacles are sharp hooks.   Yes   No

B. Next to each number, write the letter of the clue that matches it. Use the information on the other page to help you.

_____ 1. 914

_____ 2. eight

_____ 3. ten

_____ 4. three

_____ 5. two

_____ 6. 990

_____ 7. one

a. the number of tentacles that colossal squid have

b. the number of hearts that colossal squid have

c. the minimum depth in meters where the colossal squid caught in 2007 swam

d. the number of siphons that colossal squid have

e. the number of arms that colossal squid have

f. the width in inches of a colossal squid's eye

g. the weight in pounds of the colossal squid caught in 2007

Creatures of the Deep

Scientists in Antarctica are always finding new species of animals in the Southern Ocean. In 2008, researchers conducted a marine *census,* or survey, studying 30,000 animals from the deepest parts of the ocean. Hundreds of new deep-sea species were discovered.

The scientists were amazed by the great diversity of life. They were also surprised at the number of large animals they found. They discovered huge sea stars that were two feet (0.6 m) wide and jellyfish with 12-foot (4-m) tentacles. Even animals that are usually small, such as worms and sea spiders, are larger in the Southern Ocean.

Below are four unusual creatures found in the deep waters of the Southern Ocean.

Glass Tulips *Standing in fields like flowers, these creatures are actually worms that grow up to 3 feet (1 m) tall. The worms pump water through a tube in their bodies to filter out food. The water pressure holds up their "stalks."*

Sea Spider *The giant sea spider is 12 inches (30 cm) across, the size of a dinner plate. It eats by sucking fluids from its prey of small marine animals. Male sea spiders carry their eggs until they hatch.*

Sea Pig *The sea pig is not really a pig—it just looks like one. It has a fleshy body and sharp spines buried in its skin. Its mouth is surrounded by tentacles. It has tube-like feet that help it crawl along the ocean floor.*

Wart Octopus *The wart octopus has rough skin and venom that works in sub-zero temperatures. The octopus preys on large shellfish, drilling small holes in the prey's shell and injecting poisonous saliva.*

Creatures of the Deep

Answer the questions using the information on the other page to help you.

1. What did the marine census of 2008 accomplish?

   _____

   _____

2. List two things that surprised scientists during the census.

   _____

   _____

3. How are glass tulips like tulips on land? How are they different?

   _____

   _____

4. Which physical feature of the wart octopus may have had something do to with the animal's name?

   _____

5. Which is longer, a glass tulip or a giant sea spider? Write the difference in inches.

   _____

6. Which of the four creatures described on the other page would you vote for to win the "Most Unusual Animal" contest? Explain your answer.

   _____

   _____

   _____

Review

Use words from the box to complete the crossword puzzle.

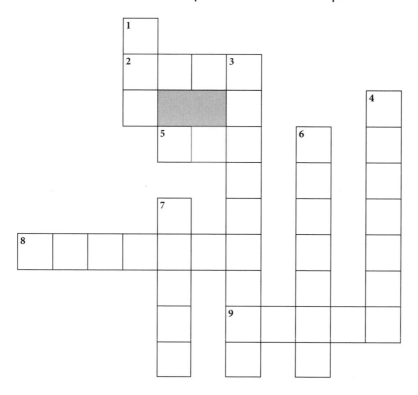

albatross

cod

emperor

krill

leopard

octopus

orca

squid

web

Across

2. The _____, or killer whale, hunts its prey in large groups.

5. Phytoplankton are at the base of the Antarctic food _____.

8. The _____ penguin is the largest penguin in Antarctica.

9. The colossal _____ has rarely been studied.

Down

1. The largest fish in Antarctica is the Antarctic _____.

3. The wandering _____ is the largest seabird in Antarctica.

4. The _____ seal is the only kind that feeds on other seals.

6. The wart _____ injects venom into its prey.

7. _____ are small shrimp-like creatures.

Assessment

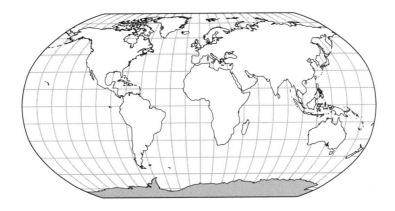

This section provides two cumulative assessments that you can use to evaluate students' acquisition of the information presented in this book. The first assessment requires students to identify landforms, bodies of water, and a research station on a map. The second assessment is a two-page multiple-choice test covering information from all sections of the book. Use one or both assessments as culminating activities for your class's study of Antarctica.

CONTENTS

Map Test

Write the name of the landform, body of water, or research station that matches each number. Use the words in the box to help you.

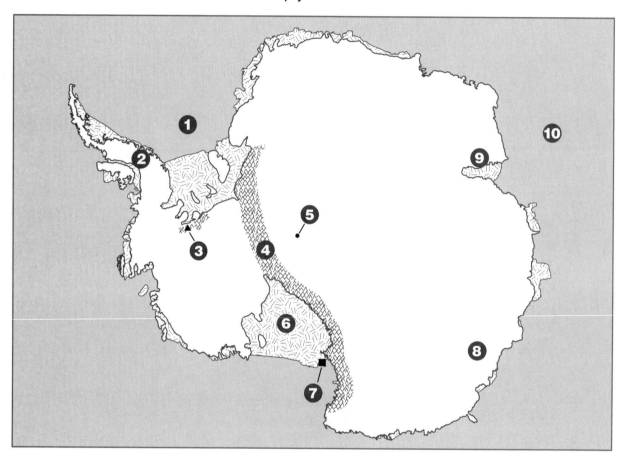

Transantarctic Mountains	**Southern Ocean**	**Ross Ice Shelf**	**South Pole**
Antarctic Peninsula	**Amery Ice Shelf**	**Weddell Sea**	**Wilkes Land**
McMurdo Station	**Vinson Massif**		

1. _____

2. _____

3. _____

4. _____

5. _____

6. _____

7. _____

8. _____

9. _____

10. _____

Multiple-Choice Test

Fill in the bubble to answer each question or complete each sentence.

1. Antarctica is the coldest, windiest, highest, and _____ continent.

   Ⓐ mildest

   Ⓑ driest

   Ⓒ dampest

   Ⓓ sandiest

2. Which important place is located in Antarctica?

   Ⓐ the equator

   Ⓑ the North Pole

   Ⓒ the South Pole

   Ⓓ the Arctic Circle

3. In which hemisphere is Antarctica *not* located?

   Ⓐ Northern

   Ⓑ Southern

   Ⓒ Eastern

   Ⓓ Western

4. The _____ is a natural border between East and West Antarctica.

   Ⓐ Ross Ice Shelf

   Ⓑ Marie Byrd Land

   Ⓒ Antarctic Peninsula

   Ⓓ Transantarctic Mountain Range

5. What is the name of the highest mountain in Antarctica?

   Ⓐ Mount Erebus

   Ⓑ Mount Terror

   Ⓒ Vinson Massif

   Ⓓ Bentley Subglacial Trench

6. What percentage of Antarctica is covered in ice?

   Ⓐ 50%

   Ⓑ 75%

   Ⓒ 89%

   Ⓓ 98%

7. Which glacier is the largest in Antarctica and the world?

   Ⓐ Mertz Glacier

   Ⓑ Lambert Glacier

   Ⓒ Mawson Glacier

   Ⓓ Amery Glacier

8. Which ocean is *not* part of the Southern Ocean?

   Ⓐ Arctic

   Ⓑ Indian

   Ⓒ Atlantic

   Ⓓ Pacific

Multiple-Choice Test

9. Which early explorer was the first to cross the Antarctic Circle?

   Ⓐ James Cook

   Ⓑ Charles Wilkes

   Ⓒ James Weddell

   Ⓓ Fabian von Bellingshausen

10. Which two explorers raced to be the first to the South Pole?

    Ⓐ Cook and Wilkes

    Ⓑ Ross and Weddell

    Ⓒ Amundsen and Scott

    Ⓓ Mawson and Shackleton

11. Which explorer was the first to fly over the South Pole?

    Ⓐ Floyd Bennett

    Ⓑ Richard E. Byrd

    Ⓒ Hubert Wilkins

    Ⓓ Lincoln Ellsworth

12. The _____ Research Station is the largest in Antarctica.

    Ⓐ Vostok

    Ⓑ Halley

    Ⓒ Casey

    Ⓓ McMurdo

13. Which penguin is the largest of the six types found in Antarctica?

    Ⓐ king

    Ⓑ gentoo

    Ⓒ emperor

    Ⓓ macaroni

14. The _____ is the largest seabird in Antarctica.

    Ⓐ seagull

    Ⓑ Adélie penguin

    Ⓒ macaroni penguin

    Ⓓ wandering albatross

15. Which animals are the most abundant in the Southern Ocean?

    Ⓐ krill

    Ⓑ seals

    Ⓒ penguins

    Ⓓ whales

16. Which two animals are at the top of the Antarctic food web?

    Ⓐ Antarctic cod and colossal squid

    Ⓑ orca and sperm whale

    Ⓒ sea spider and sea pig

    Ⓓ blue whale and leopard seal

Note Takers

This section provides four note-taker forms that give students the opportunity to culminate their study of Antarctica by doing independent research on physical features, animals, explorers, or research stations of their choice. (Some suggested topics are given below.) Students may use printed reference materials or Internet sites to gather information on their topics. A cover page is also provided so that students may create a booklet of note takers and any other reproducible pages from the book that you would like students to save.

FORMS

Name _____

Select a physical feature of Antarctica. Write notes about it to complete each section.

_____

(Name of Physical Feature)

N
W E
S

Location

_____
_____
_____
_____

Interesting Facts

_____
_____
_____
_____
_____
_____
_____
_____
_____
_____
_____
_____

Description

_____
_____
_____
_____
_____
_____
_____
_____
_____
_____

Climate

_____
_____
_____
_____

Draw an Antarctic animal. Write notes about it to complete each section.

_____

(Name of Animal)

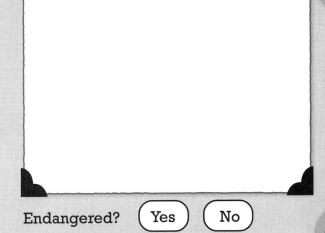

Habitat

_____
_____
_____
_____

Endangered?   (Yes)   (No)

Physical Characteristics

_____
_____
_____

Diet

_____
_____
_____
_____

Behaviors

_____
_____
_____

Enemies/Defenses

_____
_____
_____

Name _____

Select an Antarctic explorer or researcher. Write notes about him or her to complete each section.

_____

(Name of Explorer or Researcher)

From (Country)

_____

Dates of Antarctic Exploration

_____

Ship or Airplane Name

_____

Number of Expeditions

_____

N
W   E
S

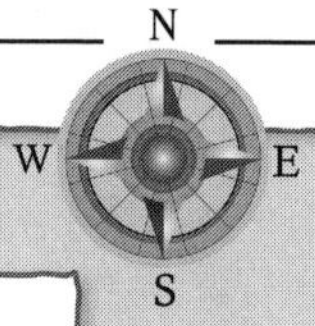

Summary of Major Expeditions

_____

_____

_____

_____

_____

_____

_____

_____

_____

_____

Important Discoveries

_____

_____

_____

Interesting Facts

_____

_____

_____

Name _____

Select an Antarctic research station. Write notes about it to complete each section.

_____

(Name of Research Station)

Owned by (Country)	Winter Population
_____	_____
Location	Summer Population
_____	_____

N
W E
S

Important Research

_____

_____

_____

_____

_____

_____

_____

_____

_____

_____

Interesting Facts

_____

_____

_____

_____

_____

_____

_____

_____

_____

_____

ANTARCTICA

Page 5

1. A   2. B   3. C   4. D   5. B

Page 6

A. South America, south, North America, Southern, Pacific

B. Students will color Australia orange, circle the Southern Ocean in blue, and draw a snake on South America.

Page 9

A. 1. c   2. f   3. h   4. e   5. j
6. b   7. g   8. i   9. a   10. d

B.

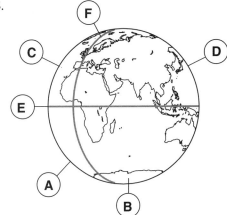

Page 11

A. 1. equator   6. latitude lines
2. prime meridian   7. 15 degrees
3. south   8. parallels
4. 75°S   9. meridians
5. 90°S

B. The Antarctic Peninsula is south of the equator and west of the prime meridian, so the latitude and longitude lines of its absolute location are labeled in degrees south and west.

Page 12

A. 1. Yes   6. Yes
2. No   7. No
3. Yes   8. No
4. Yes   9. Yes
5. No

B. A polar projection map shows land and water in relation to a central point—one of the poles.

Page 14

Across   **Down**
6. Southern   1. absolute
7. equator   2. Antarctica
8. polar   3. longitude
                 4. hemispheres
                 5. relative

Page 17

1. D   2. B   3. A   4. C   5. C

Page 19

A. 1. Pangaea   5. continent
2. Gondwana   6. Glaciers
3. Australia   7. South Pole
4. India   8. equator

B.

Page 20

A. 1. Transantarctic Mountains
2. Vinson Massif
3. South Pole
4. Mount Erebus
5. Ronne-Filchner Ice Shelf
6. Amery Ice Shelf
7. Antarctic Peninsula
8. Bentley Subglacial Trench

B. Students should color the following:

Brown: Ellsworth Mountains, Transantarctic Mountains

Gray: Amery Ice Shelf, Ronne-Filchner Ice Shelf, Ross Ice Shelf, plus all other ice shelves not labeled.

Red: South Pole

Page 23

A. 1. Yes   6. Yes
2. No   7. No
3. No   8. Yes
4. No   9. No
5. Yes   10. Yes

B. 1. Greater Antarctica
2. Amery Ice Shelf
3. plateau
4. Answers will vary—e.g., Queen Maud Land, Enderby Land, Wilkes Land

Page 25

A. 1. peak
2. Trench
3. volcano
4. Island
5. Peninsula
6. Ice Shelf
7. Ellsworth

Crack the Code!

West Antarctica is sometimes called <u>Lesser</u> Antarctica.

Page 27

A. 1. Vinson Massif   5. Ellsworth
2. Transantarctic   6. Mount Erebus
3. Transantarctic Mountains   7. Ross
4. Vinson Massif   8. Gamburtsev

B. 1. They used radar technology to find the mountains.
2. a bare peak that rises above the ice
3. a mountain range that is buried under ice
4. Carl Vinson, because he was a congressman who persuaded the U.S. to support Antarctic exploration.

Page 29

1. East Antarctica
2. 98%
3. West Antarctic ice sheet
4. George VI Sound
5. below
6. 7 million
7. to the coasts
8. a huge region of thick ice
9. They were formed from layers of snow that were pressed together over millions of years.
10. A glacier is a mass of slowly moving ice. A valley glacier is a glacier that flows through the valleys between mountains.

Page 31

A. 1. b   4. a
2. d   5. f
3. e   6. c

B. An ice shelf is a wide, thick platform of ice that extends onto the ocean's surface. An iceberg is a block of freshwater ice that breaks off an ice shelf and floats in the ocean.

C. An ice sheet can flow down to the coastline and extend onto the ocean's surface, becoming an ice shelf. Then, a piece of ice can calve off the ice shelf, becoming an iceberg.

Page 32

A.

```
S O U T H E R N C H E U L U Q
A E G J N A I B A R L O Q A C
N F P R Y D Z S V L J T C C G
G W M A I V H R E F L I H U M
T K V Z T N H D R I F O D Q C
Z A A U G S D N D I I F U F M
E M V L W E T A C L W L Q S U
J U K J W F C I V U W A L F M
Y N K E Y S L P A I L A K G C
R D R U S R J S Y H S F T N M
V S W O V O S T O K G K C A U
N E R E A R S C A E K F A G R
K N V I V O S K O T L G A X D
D K T S N G A O L H J Q A P O
```

B. Students should circle using the following colors:

Blue: Amundsen Sea, Bellingshausen Sea, Davis Sea, Dumont d'Urville Sea, Ross Sea, Scotia Sea, Weddell Sea

Red: Lutzow-Holm Bay, Prydz Bay

Green: Cape Poinsett, George VI Sound, McMurdo Sound

Page 35

A. 1. interior   6. coastal areas
2. coastal areas   7. peninsula
3. peninsula   8. coastal areas
4. interior   9. coastal areas
5. peninsula   10. interior

B. the Antarctic Peninsula because temperatures are the warmest there

Page 37

A. 1. Antarctic Peninsula
   2. about 10
   3. Larsen Ice Shelf
   4. Southern Ocean
   5. a layer of ozone gas that is part of Earth's atmosphere
   6. protects Earth from dangerous ultraviolet radiation from the sun
   7. September–December
   8. pollution from synthetic chemicals

B. Warming could cause ocean levels to rise and endanger coastal cities, and decreased ozone levels could allow harmful radiation to cause damage to plants, animals, and people.

Page 38

Across	Down
1. Trench	2. continent
4. Southern	3. Mountains
7. Lambert	5. sheets
8. Ross	6. Pangaea
9. peak	

Page 41

1. B   2. A   3. C   4. A   5. D

Page 43

1. unknown southern land
2. Ferdinand Magellan
3. 1773
4. New Zealand
5. 70 miles
6. opposite the Bear
7. that it would be inhabited and have rich soil
8. that they could only be caused by thick ice that came from a landmass
9. because it was a place that had terrible storms, bitterly cold winds, and large amounts of ice

Page 45

A. 1. No   6. Yes
   2. No   7. No
   3. Yes   8. Yes
   4. Yes   9. Yes
   5. No   10. Yes

B. They wanted to claim land for their countries, hunt seals and whales, and make new scientific discoveries.

Page 47

A. 1. **Bellingshausen:** to get as close as possible to the unknown southern land
      Weddell: to hunt seals for their skins
   2. **Bellingshausen:** Antarctic Peninsula, Peter I Island, Alexander I Island
      Weddell: Weddell seals, George IV Sea (Weddell Sea)

B. Students should circle using the following colors:

   Yellow: Alexander I Island, Antarctic Peninsula, Bellingshausen Sea, Peter I Island

   Green: South Orkney Islands, Weddell Sea

Page 49

Answers will vary—e.g.,
1. What was the absolute location of the Magnetic South Pole in 1841? About 76°S latitude, 160°E longitude.
2. How many degrees of latitude was Ross from the Geographic South Pole? 12 degrees.

Page 51

1. e   6. d
2. b   7. g
3. f   8. c
4. i   9. a
5. h

Page 53

A. 1. Amundsen   5. Scott
   2. Shackleton   6. Mawson
   3. Mawson   7. Amundsen
   4. Scott   8. Shackleton

B. Answers will vary—e.g., Bravery because you need to be brave to explore the icy cold continent of Antarctica, and intelligence because you have to be smart to figure out where you are going and how to get back home.

Page 55

A. 1. Mawson   6. Mawson
   2. Shackleton   7. Shackleton
   3. Shackleton   8. Mawson
   4. Shackleton   9. Mawson
   5. Mawson   10. Shackleton

B. Answers will vary—e.g., Yes, because they both had to survive dangerous expeditions. Shackleton saved many lives during his journey and Mawson had to fend for himself when his companions died.

Page 59

Ship's name:
Amundsen: the *Fram*
Scott: the *Terra Nova*

Country and date:
Amundsen: Norway, August 9, 1910
Scott: the United Kingdom, June 1, 1910

Base camp:
Amundsen: Bay of Whales, 2 miles inland
Scott: Cape Evans

Date expedition begins:
Amundsen: October 20, 1911
Scott: November 1, 1911

Names of men chosen:
Amundsen: Bjaaland, Hanssen, Hassel, and Wisting
Scott: Bowers, Evans, Oates, and Wilson

Two obstacles or tragedies: (Answers will vary)
Amundsen: 24 dogs have to be killed, the men are frostbitten
Scott: motorized sledges fail, ponies die

Date of arrival:
Amundsen: December 14, 1911
Scott: January 17, 1912

Description of return journey:
Amundsen: Amundsen, his 4 men, and 11 dogs take 39 days to return to base camp. They sail home on the *Fram*.
Scott: Scott and his men encounter blizzard conditions and become badly frostbitten. They die from the cold, waiting out a blizzard in their tent.

Page 61

A. 1. balloon
   2. Wilkins
   3. Ellsworth
   4. airplanes
   5. helicopters
   6. South Pole
   7. High Jump
   8. photographs

B. Answers will vary—e.g., Operation High Jump because the aerial photographs helped mapmakers figure out the coastline of Antarctica.

Page 63

A. 5, 2, 7, 3, 6, 1, 4

B. 1. for being the first to fly over the North Pole
   2. operating an advanced base camp in Antarctica himself for the winter

C. Answers will vary—e.g., leading operation High Jump because he was in charge of such a large expedition

Page 64

Across	Down
2. Island	1. Unknown
4. Scott	3. South Pole
5. Heroic	6. seal
7. *Belgica*	7. Byrd

Page 67

1. A   2. D   3. B   4. C   5. D

Page 69

A. 1. for scientists around the world to study Earth and share their findings
   2. 12 countries; more than 50 stations
   3. Argentina, Australia, Chile, France, New Zealand, Norway, the United Kingdom
   4. to settle territorial claims and provide guidelines for how Antarctica should be used in the future

B. 1. No   4. No
   2. Yes   5. Yes
   3. Yes   6. No

Page 71

1. summer
2. Amundsen-Scott, McMurdo, Palmer
3. near the South Pole
4. United States and Russia
5. United States and New Zealand
6. near the Amery Ice Shelf
7. Australia and Russia
8. Antarctica is dark six months of the year, which makes it ideal to study space. Also, its ice helps scientists study and understand global climate change.

Page 73

A. Answers will vary—e.g.,
   1. Who was McMurdo Station named after? Lieutenant Archibald McMurdo, who was on Ross's ship, the *Terror*, in 1841.
   2. What are three ways that people can come and go to and from McMurdo Station? By ship at the harbor, by airplane at the airfields, and by helicopter at the helipad.
   3. What can people do for fun at "Mac Town"? They can go shopping, listen to the radio, watch TV, or go to the gym.

B. 1. b   2. f   3. e   4. c   5. a   6. d

Page 75

Students should write an article that contains information about the four-woman team from Ohio State University, their work in the McMurdo Dry Valleys, and how their expedition helped open doors for future female scientists.

Page 77

1. hour
2. longitude
3. twenty-four
4. Vostok
5. Standard

Crack the Code!

Many stations in Antarctica do not use <u>daylight savings</u> time.

Page 79

A. 1. h 2. f 3. d 4. c 5. a
   6. i 7. j 8. b 9. g 10. e

B. 1. Scientists can transmit data to their home countries.
   2. Communication satellites provide cellular and Internet service.
   3. Satellites allow radio stations, TV stations, and newspapers to transmit their news electronically.

Page 81

A. 1. Yes   6. No
   2. Yes   7. Yes
   3. No   8. Yes
   4. Yes   9. No
   5. No   10. Yes

B. An oil spill from a large ship could pollute Antarctic waters. Tourists could disturb the habitat of Antarctic wildlife.

Page 82

Across	Down
1. tourists	2. summer
4. time	3. McMurdo
5. research	6. satellites
7. women	
8. Antarctic	

Page 85

1. C   2. C   3. B   4. A   5. D

Page 87

A. 1. krill
   2. leopard seal
   3. blue whale
   4. orcas and leopard seals
   5. phytoplankton and plant-eating zooplankton
   6. orcas and sperm whales
   7. Five; seabirds, leopard seals, penguins, elephant seals, and squid
   8. fish, plant-eating zooplankton, and krill

B. A food chain is one group of living things shown in the order in which each member feeds on another one. A food web is a collection of overlapping and connected food chains.

Page 89

A. 1. crustacean
   2. phytoplankton
   3. predator
   4. translucent
   5. thousand
   6. swarms

B. Students should trace a large paper clip and then draw a krill of about the same size. Then they should complete the caption. Captions will vary— e.g., Antarctic krill are about 2 inches (5 cm) long.

Page 91

A. 1. 11 feet (3 m)
   2. squid and fish
   3. 5,000
   4. at sea
   5. a fledgling
   6. Parents take turns sitting on the eggs and they fly great distances to find food for their chicks.

B. 1. because killing the albatross cursed the ship
   2. Answers will vary—e.g., *Pinocchio*: Every time Pinocchio lied, his nose grew a little longer.

Page 93

1. Answers will vary—e.g., They all have beaks and they all have black and white feathers.
2. Answers will vary—e.g., The macaroni penguin has fluffy feathers above its eyes and the chinstrap doesn't. The chinstrap has a white face and the macaroni has a black face.

Page 95

A. **Adélie Penguin:** smallest penguin in Antarctica; white ring around eyes; reddish beak; eats krill; builds nests with small stones; female lays 2 eggs

Emperor Penguin: largest penguin in Antarctica; blackish-blue body; patches of white and yellow around ears and neck; eats crab and lobster; has no nest; female lays one egg

Both: eat fish and squid; enemies are leopard seals, killer whales, and seabirds

B. Students should draw either an Adélie or emperor penguin and complete the caption. Captions will vary—e.g., Emperor penguins are 42 inches (115 cm) tall and weigh 84 pounds (38 kg).

Page 99

A.
1. leopard seal
2. fur seal
3. Ross seal
4. elephant seal
5. leopard seal
6. crabeater seal
7. fur seal
8. Weddell seal
9. Weddell seal
10. elephant seal

B. Answers will vary—e.g., The southern elephant seal because it has a trunk-like snout that inflates, it can bend its body in a U shape while fighting, and is very large.

Page 101

A.
```
A N B F I S D E E J R C B A B
B E W H S H R H M G W H C T O
M S Q U I D E U L O C R J L T
C R A L E M T M A P O A S Y T
D E I Z L V A P M E O B E X L
A C W O A H B B A L E E N H E
U A B S H L E A T I H H W B N
O L I N A M Z C J T P S E T O
P F G P L F I K R I L L E G S
A I X E K U K L N O I D Z E
X S E U N T O O T H E D H O
P D L U W A G F I S E K R V C
R B N W M X C U K P O N V H E
Y A T E V J U P I T E S S A
M V E H Z E G U L N U M X A D
```

B. Answers will vary—e.g.,
1. There are 11 species of whales in the Southern Ocean—six are baleen and five are toothed.
2. The humpback whale is a baleen whale known for its long, singing call.
3. The orca is a toothed whale that hunts large prey, such as blue whale calves, in groups.

Page 103

1. adapted
2. dormant
3. crocodile
4. icefish
5. proteins
6. bladder

Crack the Code!
Three kinds of fish mentioned on the other page are *piscivorous* (peh-SIV-eh-ruhs), which means they are <u>fish eaters</u>.

Page 105

A.
1. Yes
2. No
3. Yes
4. No
5. No
6. Yes
7. Yes
8. Yes

B. 1. c   2. e   3. f   4. b   5. a   6. g   7. d

Page 107

1. Scientists studied 30,000 animals from the deep sea and discovered hundreds of new species.
2. They were surprised at the diversity of life and the number of large animals they found.
3. They stand in fields like flowers and they look like tulips, but they are actually worms.
4. its rough skin
5. a glass tulip is 24 inches longer
6. Answers will vary—e.g., The sea pig because it looks like a creepy version of a regular pig, has tentacles around its mouth, and sharp spines buried in its skin.

Page 108

Across	Down
2. orca	1. cod
5. web	3. albatross
8. emperor	4. leopard
9. squid	6. octopus
	7. krill

Page 110

1. Weddell Sea
2. Antarctic Peninsula
3. Vinson Massif
4. Transantarctic Mountains
5. South Pole
6. Ross Ice Shelf
7. McMurdo Station
8. Wilkes Land
9. Amery Ice Shelf
10. Southern Ocean

Page 111

1. B   2. C   3. A   4. D   5. C   6. D   7. B   8. A

Page 112

9. A   10. C   11. B   12. D   13. C   14. D   15. A   16. B

WEEK 31

Daily Geography

Sampler
Daily Geography Practice
Grade 5 • Week 31

Skill: Cooperative Solutions
Essential Element 4: Standard 13

Time Zones of the United States

Introducing the Map

Ask students what it would be like if every community in the United States used a different time. The obvious answer is that people would be confused and many problems would be created. To avoid this confusion, a cooperative system was designed called *standard time zones*. Talk about the advantages of having regional time zones.

Explain the concept of time zones. A day is 24 hours long—the time it takes Earth to complete one rotation on its axis. Earth is divided into 24 time zones. The United States is divided into six of those twenty-four time zones.

Show students the Time Zones of the United States map. Tell students that each zone uses a time one hour different from its neighboring zones. The hours are earlier to the west of each zone and later to the east.

Go over all the names of the time zones and have students notice the one hour difference between each of them. Talk about how Alaska is so large that it covers two time zones. Explain that some of the Aleutian Islands of Alaska are so far west that scientists placed them with Hawaii, thus creating Hawaiian-Aleutian Time.

Ask students which time zone Chicago, Illinois, is in. They will probably say Central Time. Then ask them: If it is 3:00 P.M. in Chicago, what time is it in Denver? The answer is 2:00 P.M. Ask students a couple more questions, each time changing the local times to help students understand the concept.

Extend the lesson to discuss daylight saving time. This is a plan in which clocks are set one hour ahead of standard time for a certain period of time. The plan provides for an additional hour of daylight. It begins on the first Sunday in April and ends on the last Sunday in October. Most states choose to go on daylight saving time, but several don't. Talk about how that complicates things.

Introducing Vocabulary

daylight saving time a plan in which clocks are set one hour ahead of standard time for a specific period of time

standard time zone a region in which the same time is used

time zone a region in which the same time is used; Earth is divided into 24 time zones

ANSWER KEY

Note: Not all questions can be answered with information from the map. Students will have to use their mental map skills to locate places on the map.

Monday
1. 6; Hawaiian-Aleutian, Alaskan, Pacific, Mountain, Central, and Eastern Times
2. one hour

Tuesday
1. earlier
2. Eastern Time

Wednesday
1. Hawaiian-Aleutian Time
2. 11:00 A.M.

Thursday
1. 10:00 P.M.
2. North Dakota, South Dakota, Nebraska, Kansas, and Texas

Friday
1. No, it's 2:00 A.M. and Grandfather is probably sleeping.
2. It is Daylight Saving Time.

Challenge
Answers will vary, but students should make up two questions and provide answers to the questions.

Time Zones of the United States

Daylight Saving Time begins on the first Sunday in April and ends on the last Sunday in October. Remember this trick to set your clocks one hour ahead in the spring and one hour back in the fall: *Spring ahead; Fall back.*

New York

Chicago

Denver

Los Angeles

Juneau

Honolulu

4:00 P.M.
Eastern Time

3:00 P.M.
Central Time

2:00 P.M.
Mountain Time

1:00 P.M.
Pacific Time

12:00 P.M.
Alaskan Time

11:00 A.M.
Hawaiian-Aleutian Time

Name _____

Time Zones of the United States

Monday

1. The United States is divided into how many standard time zones? Name them from west to east.

   _____

   _____

   _____

2. What is the time difference between each neighboring time zone?

   _____

Tuesday

1. Are the hours earlier or later to the west of each time zone?

   _____

2. Cities in the Northeast region are part of which time zone?

   _____

Wednesday

1. Which time zone includes Hawaii and some of the western islands of Alaska?

   _____

2. If it is 1:00 P.M. in Chicago, what time is it in Los Angeles?

   _____

Time Zones of the United States

Thursday

1. If it is midnight in Chicago, what time is it in Seattle, Washington?

_____

2. Which states have areas that are part of Central and Mountain Time Zones?

_____

_____

_____

Friday

1. If you live in Honolulu and it is 9:00 P.M., is it a good time to call your grandfather in New York? Why or why not?

_____

_____

2. It is the first Sunday in April and clocks have been set one hour ahead. Why?

_____

Challenge

Make up two time zone questions. Write your questions on the back of the map. Don't forget to include the answer. Pair up with a classmate and ask each other the time zone questions.